STILLWATER
STRATEGIES

STILLWATER STRATEGIES

7 Practical Lessons
for Catching More Fish
in Lakes, Reservoirs,
and Ponds

TIM LOCKHART

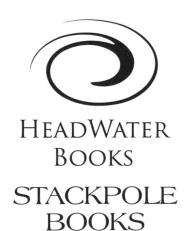

HEADWATER
BOOKS

STACKPOLE
BOOKS

Published by

STACKPOLE BOOKS
5067 Ritter Road
Mechanicsburg, PA 17055
www.stackpolebooks.com

Printed in the United States

First edition

10 9 8 7 6 5 4 3 2 1

Library of Congress Cataloging-in-Publication Data

Lockhart, Tim.
    Stillwater strategies : 7 practical lessons for catching more fish in lakes, reservoirs, and ponds / Tim Lockhart. — First edition.
        pages   cm
    Includes index.
    ISBN 978-0-8117-1137-1 (pbk.)
    1. Trout fishing. 2. Fly fishing. I. Title.

    SH687.L56 2013
    799.1757—dc23

                                                             2012026431

In memory of Don Ward, Nish Samoulian,
and other anglers forever missed on the water

Contents

Acknowledgments

First I would like to thank Jay Nichols at Stackpole Books for giving me a shot as a new author. Jay's guidance and editing talent made this book possible, and I am grateful for everything I learned from him along the way.

Next I'd like to thank Christian Brewer, who convinced me to do this. Christian saw the potential well before I did and has been a major source of help and advice throughout.

Thanks also to Roy Spradlin for a lot of inspiration and ideas shared on the water. For much of the time spent gaining the experience behind this book, Roy was the guy fishing next to me.

Many thanks to Corky Johnson, who gave me my first fly rod and a swift kick in this direction.

Special thanks to my brother, Jeff, for his great enthusiasm and support. Jeff has always been there for me.

Introduction

When it comes to lake fishing, any fly fisher can show up during prime conditions and catch trout left and right. An abundant hatch, ideal temperatures, and minimal angling pressure would be nice every time out—if only our sport worked that way. Yet, on a whim, the sport can show a rather difficult and more realistic side, leaving you and me with more questions than answers. Trout react to a wide variation in conditions, and the angler must commit to understanding the countless factors that influence when and where activity will occur.

This book was written to guide you through the entire process of stillwater fly fishing—first by identifying what matters and then by prioritizing all the elements in order of relevance. In presenting the material this way, I am calling attention to the adverse impact of focusing on only part of the equation, or of placing too much emphasis on the wrong priorities. Conversely, I'm also trying to emphasize the significant benefits of assembling the puzzle pieces in meaningful and logical order every time out. More importantly, when you hit one of those difficult days, you'll be ready with a game plan—and the confidence to keep finding and catching fish.

This book also teaches and encourages open-mindedness and creative thought, encouraging a freedom that goes a long way in the complex and often chaotic stillwater environment. My hope is that you will walk away with a very useful set of tools for solving any puzzle that may present itself, and that the book will remain a solid reference as time goes on.

As fly fishers, we've been wired to think our chosen nymph, streamer, or Chironomid pattern is the sole—or most important—factor for whatever happens on the water. I'd love to tell you that's all there is to it. But while fly selection can be an important part of the game, successful angling on lakes requires a whole lot more. In this book, I identify what really matters when pursuing trout in stillwater.

In Lesson 1, I introduce the basic set of priorities to be followed throughout the book; I also discuss ways to find the most promising stillwater locations—the foundation for success. In Lesson 2, I talk about how to locate trout in a lake by focusing on the various factors that influence their activity. Of all of the skills you can bring to an outing, your ability to determine WHEN and WHERE fish are likely to be active will be the most important by far. In fact, that skill is the essential focus of this book.

Once you learn how to select a good lake and figure out where the fish are, you'll need a few tricks up your sleeve to outsmart them. Lesson 3 provides exactly that—introducing you to a number of productive ways to present your fly. We'll talk about how to draw strikes in a variety of different circumstances, as well as the most effective ways to land your fish once hooked.

Lesson 4 describes how to dissect a lake to identify characteristics relevant to successful fly fishing. I pick apart the elements of my example lake piece by piece—and explain how you can develop the same in-depth knowledge for any body of stillwater. A comprehensive familiarity with at least one location will get you more fish and result in a better angling education than anything else could. It's the fly fisher's version of home-field advantage.

After that, you'll be ready to go out, get wet, and put it all into practice. Lesson 5, "Anatomy of an Outing," walks you through an entire day on the water, explaining every decision and its outcome in detail. This lesson is based on an actual fly-fishing experience and brings to life a lot of the material presented to this point.

Finally, Lessons 6 and 7 review two opposing scenarios common in stillwater fly fishing: slow days and very active days. I discuss ways to get the best results under either circumstance, as well as identify some of the pitfalls to avoid. We'll also see what a best-case outing should look like in each situation.

Throughout the book, after first discussing the various concepts and principles, I illustrate how they would apply in a variety of scenarios. I talk about the different ways that both success and failure can be determined in a single day—and the degree to which certain decisions can directly impact your results. By the end of the book, you should have a good working knowledge of the nature of trout, how each of a long list of factors affects trout behavior, and ultimately WHEN and WHERE trout can be found.

Remember: In successful fly fishing, you are only one-half of the equation; the trout is the other half.

In addition to knowing what affects your target's whereabouts, you should also have proficiency in observation, interpretation, decision making, execution, time management, and other skills that help you to determine both the elements of your pursuit and which tools to employ.

While most of my experience in stillwater fly fishing comes from the US Pacific Northwest, which has its own unique set of conditions, I believe most of the techniques in this book will hold true across the country or abroad. Fly fishers use a wide variety of techniques and face varying circumstances worldwide; however, the same principles apply in terms of trout behavior, effective search methods, and prioritizing elements of the approach.

If you learn only one thing from this book, understand that your fly selection is the last priority, behind all the factors that determine whether that fly gets in front of a fish or not. Put simply, the most brilliantly tied fly will get you nothing if presented in empty water; however, most anything in your box will draw strike after strike when presented skillfully in plain view of active trout. Successful lake angling means you have to look beyond the fly. Well beyond it.

After reading this book, your obvious next step will be to get out there and put these ideas into practice. In terms of learning, I compare fly fishing to playing a musical instrument: Good instruction is essential, but your progress is more a function of the time spent practicing, failing, and working through frustrations along the way. Even if you consider yourself a new or less experienced fly fisher, with time and patience you will find yourself getting it right and growing in confidence, little by little. This sport is for everyone who wants to pursue it, and I have yet to meet a good fly fisher who regrets having put in the work to succeed.

Over time, Mother Nature's elusive trout really has not changed. Today's trout behavior and habits would probably have been the same a hundred or even a thousand years ago. What has changed is our understanding of what affects trout behavior—and our skills to give chase with rod and reel. Every year, I find myself fishing a little differently than the year before—and with better results. My hope is that this will continue to happen until I can no longer fish and, along the way, that I will be able to assist as many others as I can in the same endeavor. I might always fish for the same reasons, but the methods I use will continue to evolve, keeping it as interesting as ever.

Stillwater fly fishing is anything but an exact science, and I call that a very good thing. If what I call the classic school of thought—concerning pattern selection, execution methods, fly-casting techniques, and such— were the only means to achievement, I'd get skunked every time. The real beauty in all of it is that you and I can bring to our sport as much innovation as we can dream up—because the trout is a living creature with a certain unpredictability in both behavior and movement. In my experience, the aptitude to respond creatively—to willingly follow trout into unexpected places—is the key to wearing a hole in your net faster than anything else.

Best of luck!

Lesson 1

FINDING QUALITY LAKES

My fundamental formula or method for stillwater fly fishing is simple: WHEN–WHERE–HOW–WHAT, in that order. That's the sequence I've developed over 35 years on the water. Every single one of the subtle details I outline in this book fits into those four priorities, and keeping the formula in that sequence is about the only rule that I follow religiously.

So I'll start with a discussion on how to locate water of good quality for fly fishing. Further along, I'll talk about how to locate and draw fish on a specific body of water—but first let's find the body of water.

We all have our own preferences when it comes to lakes and ponds. Size, seclusion, and scenery all factor in, but we can all agree on the following: Fish need to be present, and we need to be able to catch them. The technique I am about to describe has proven successful for me over a number of years and should apply to any type of stillwater.

Beyond the usual outings with friends and general exploration for fun, I keep a small "portfolio" of quality fishing spots that suit my own preferences, small (or few) being the key.

Of those, I keep close track of two lowland lakes that I know very well; another two or three lowland lakes that I watch less closely; four small, mid-elevation lakes; and another four of the same that I'm less committed to. The spots that I visit less often have proven great as backups to my main sites; occasionally one will get hot, and I'll give it more focus for a while. I limit myself to just enough lakes and ponds that I can get to regularly, so I can maintain a good working knowledge of each in terms of cycles, activity, and other characteristics.

These locations don't all produce at the same time, but if I watch, say, a dozen in total, I know that about half of them will provide good fishing at any given time. For example, in some years, one spot may be overrun with stockers, and many of the earlier plants may have disappeared. I see that this location is between cycles, so I'll spend less time there until the next cycle comes around. In a season or two, it may overflow with 14- to 16-inch cutts or whatever; then I'm all over it. I won't kid you, it can take a long time, even years, to develop a good list of lakes, but once you have it, you'll be able to spend virtually all of your time catching fish. You'll also understand how to select new spots to add to your list, if necessary, and even how to find good stillwater fishing sites while traveling.

My selections include lowland and mid-elevation lakes in the Pacific Northwest where I live. Elevation and other factors may be much different in your area, requiring a different set of criteria for assembling your "watch list."

Lowland lakes and reservoirs are attractive to fly fishers for a number of reasons that I will outline; however, the majority of this lesson focuses on the lesser known, more difficult to reach water out there.

FISHING LOWLAND WATERS

Lowland waters are fairly straightforward, given their easy access and the availability of information, so it's less a matter of research than of choosing a location that offers what you like. For example, I look for lakes that have brown trout, catch-and-release regulations, good variation of terrain and cover, and a year-round fishing season, and that are a reasonable distance from home. Examples of other common criteria: easy boat access, other amenities, stocks that excel in size or numbers, level of upkeep or limited abuse, reasonable safety for night fishing. In my case, I'm mostly looking for good quality, consistent producers that provide sufficient sport for most of the year. I am therefore willing to bend on things like scenery, seclusion, and noise factors, since I include those elements in my other group of more secluded lakes.

This does not mean lowland waters are less desirable than those that are more secluded; lowland lakes simply offer their own unique benefits and experiences. For starters, convenient year-round access means better availability for practice, learning, teaching, and camaraderie. In fact, for most of us, the majority of the time we spend fishing will be on these waters because of our busy schedules, seasonal constraints, and other life factors. Fortunately, fishing is perfectly good on these waters.

Proficiency gained from time invested on one or two lowland lakes will serve an angler better than attempting to follow the action everywhere. Visit as many waters as you like, but be sure and have some home turf where your knowledge and skills can develop. If phrases like "It's just nice to be out here today" are getting on your nerves, having your own reliable fishing waters will certainly help.

On the other hand, because of their accessibility, lowland lakes also have some potential downsides. Be wary of lakes known for big openers. These may receive significant plants each year, but they are often largely fished out within the first few weeks of the season. Take part in those early weeks if you're new to stillwater angling, but expect the fun to be short-lived. You'll want to pursue different waters for the rest of the year.

A number of otherwise good lakes can be spoiled by the crowds they attract and the activities that take place there. In lowland lakes you usually can't avoid problems altogether, but some places are definitely worse than others. When a lake regularly draws large numbers for power boating, jet skiing, and other recreational water sports, you're best off passing it by in favor of waters more suited for angling.

Pay attention to your local state stocking reports. Besides knowing how area lakes are planted, you'll eventually gain a good sense of which lakes are the better prospects. Moreover, you'll start to recognize which lakes have balanced populations and which have been overstocked. Lakes that receive too many plants are among the least desirable to fish; generally they'll have a lot of small trout that are far too easy to catch, and you'll lose interest fast. I rarely encounter lakes that are inadequately stocked. When the population is low, it's usually an issue of too much pressure, or something about a lake's conditions that won't allow trout to thrive: other species, lack of food, and less-than-ideal terrain are examples.

FISHING LESS PRESSURED WATER
Hidden stillwater can include a variety of mid- or upper-elevation lakes, reservoirs and ponds. These more secluded waters may be more difficult to reach, but they offer their own special rewards. Generally, it's easier to find fish in these waters than in lowland lakes. While you will continue to apply your own subjective criteria in selecting hidden waters, now you'll want to put more focus on finding fishable locations; that's where the real effort comes in.

Though these hidden stillwaters tend to fish more easily, you need the skill to discover their secrets by fishing them properly. Otherwise, it's far too easy to pass right over a potential honey hole simply because you lack the ability to draw fish out.

Some of the lakes and ponds I frequent have remained unspoiled because most fishers who show up don't have the experience to fish them effectively. Many are hikers who had seen the lake before and thought they'd come back and give it a try. In my years of prospecting hidden waters, I've only run across two or three people who were as serious about it as I was. Having to use your shoes to get to water is a beautiful thing—and perhaps the best way of ensuring the quality of your favored spots.

PROSPECTING FOR YOUR LIST OF STILLWATER
I think of prospecting as a two-step process involving profiling and leg work.

Profiling
Profiling is the act of narrowing down your choices to fit a handful of predetermined factors. The factors I use come from my own experience. They include timing, elevation, accessibility (requiring hiking or climbing, not accessible by car, or possessing other barriers to human traffic), lake size/acreage, low stocking count, fertile environment, balanced fish popula-

tion, travel/hiking distance, and any signs of fishing pressure. Over time, this combination has yielded consistent results—a very high probability of success when a lake or pond fits within most or all of these parameters. Let's look at each in specific detail.

Timing. Timing is everything. Remember, as I said at the beginning of this chapter, the order of criteria is important: WHEN comes before WHERE. This year's premier honey hole will produce exactly the same as that over-fished lake down the road if you don't time it right. Many conditions determine trout activity, temperature and food being the two primary drivers. Generally, at mid-elevation, you can fish most or all of the year in western Washington, as long as temperatures and weather conditions are not extreme. I recommend looking for water temperatures in the 45- to 65-degree F range, the closer to 55 degrees, the better. And when you hear that spring and fall are generally the best times for catching trout, this is why: Those are the seasons when water temperatures tend to be most comfortable for the fish, and the more comfortable the water temperature, the more active the trout become. More on this later.

Mid-Elevation. You may not be able to include elevation as a factor in your choice of water, depending on your region's topography, but where it applies, I recommend taking it into consideration. Mid-elevation affords a nice general protection against overuse while still allowing a fertile environment. I have found mid-elevation fish to grow surprisingly large, enjoying an environment similar to that of lowland lakes, while being largely left alone by would-be anglers. I can't offer a hard-and-fast rule for altitude since conditions vary in different areas, but I generally stay within the range of one thousand to two thousand feet. It's just enough.

Footwork Required. I repeat, this is a beautiful thing. A trail or gated road is a must, and if the route goes uphill, so do your odds. A mid-elevation location alone cannot ensure protection. If your local US Forest Service Road passes within sight of the pond you're considering, leave the gear home and bring a garbage bag instead. Oh, and forget that nice healthy stock of fish.

Other Barriers. These can include anything that keeps crowds out. Use your imagination because many things can serve as barriers: steep or rugged terrain, swamp or mud, wetlands, washouts, even lack of information. Many small lakes and ponds simply aren't listed anywhere, or can be found only in very obscure references. It can be well worth your time to track down bodies of water that are not listed as lakes or that seem unlikely

Mid-elevation angling provides a good balance of seclusion and fertile habitat. A high-elevation lake can also provide unparalleled fishing; however, limited season, a more challenging commute, and other conditions will often make it a difficult prospect.

to have a fish population. Granted, it's tough to score on these long shots, but if you do, it's pure gold—and it's all yours. With some effort you'll develop an eye for the unseen and less obvious factors that can help to protect your chosen water.

Size/Acreage. The smaller the better. I generally look for bodies of water with an area of under twenty acres—preferably less than ten. Some of my best spots are even an acre or two. Why? For one thing, I can cover the entire body of water every time out and become familiar with every square foot of its terrain. Second, on the whole, smaller lakes tend to show good probability for success. They just do.

How does a pond differ from a lake? I consider a pond to be simply a small lake commonly, but not always, found in a secluded, often scenic, area. Many ponds are just an acre or two. Beyond that, I don't see the use in drilling down to a more detailed definition. I've discovered good ponds in some pretty unusual places, yet they supported trout. If you can manage

Foot planks are occasionally found in parklands and other well-kept areas. Enjoy luxuries like these when you can, but always prepare for less convenient routes when exploring.

Who says trout can't get fat in small ponds? With enough food, the right conditions, and little to no fishing pressure, fish can thrive in these environments.

to see the world in terms of possibilities, you may make some pretty surprising discoveries of your own.

Low-End Stocking Count. Everyone looks for monster stocking reports. Thirty thousand must be good, right? Fifty thousand even better, right? I recommend going the other way on this one. Look for dumps of less than five hundred. There are two great reasons to take a contrarian approach on this. First, it's under the radar, and second, no one considers a simple ratio like fish-per-acre. A fish dump of two hundred means they went into a bathtub—a small, more obscure body of water—not Lake Erie. And guess what happens when most, or all, of those two hundred are left to grow.

Fertile Environment. Where I live, most lakes fit into this category. Still, your evaluation of a potential lake always must consider food and conditions. Not every body of water affords its inhabitants a good year-round supply of food along with sufficient cover, vegetation, and other conditions necessary to sustain a good, balanced population. Put another way—can they get big in there? Consider the general area you're about to explore, and then spend the day making on-site observations. Some indicators of fertility to look for include the following:

With secluded lakes and ponds, a scene such as this and no other anglers can go hand in hand much of the time. It can give new meaning to the word "loneliness."

- **Subsurface vegetation that appears healthy and balanced:** I've seen lakes with practically none and also with too much to the point of being choked out; neither is good.
- **Reasonable amounts of shade and cover:** These can be both in and around the water.
- **Appearance of visible food sources:** Again, do they appear balanced versus scarce or overpopulated?
- **Anything else that may affect a trout habitat:** This could be anything from an uncommon food source to mistreatment of the environment/water quality by humans. Overall, you don't need to be a trained expert to make some observations about the likelihood of a healthy and fertile environment for trout. A little common sense goes a long way here.

Balanced Population. This is where a little skill and experience begin to pay off. Fly fishers need enough ability and confidence to determine not just that good fish exist in a body of water, but that the population is healthy and balanced. Many locations won't support a generation of larger, older fish. Many lakes and ponds can easily become overpopulated; watch

Cover is anywhere fish can hide: fallen trees, submerged structure, brushy shorelines, and so on. When you see this much of it you're on the right track.

for this where brook trout live, since they tend to overproduce more than other species. As you watch a location over time, beware of, say, a small pond with an overwhelming abundance of 7-inch fish. On the other hand, when you start seeing them in the 14-inch range, it's generally a very good sign. The optimum site is water that allows fish to grow into the upper teens with regularity and won't say no to 20-plus-inch growth. And that includes cutthroat. They exist at that size and do quite nicely in small still-water bodies.

Furthermore, I recommend tracking the population and sizes of fish in your sites from year to year. Whatever you encounter in that first year will likely grow predictably in subsequent years, assuming the pond is not over-populated. Once planted, fish start to get interesting after about three years. They get really interesting in about five years. Start paying attention to stocking reports for the waters you fish and you'll see what I mean. Further, the rate of trout growth in many low- to mid-elevation ponds can be stag-geringly rapid compared to that in an average lowland lake.

Distance from Home and Rig. I consider these factors to be as impor-tant to my selection as the other criteria. A major part of good fishing is frequency, or time spent at a single location. My rule of thumb is an hour's drive plus an hour's hike. For lowland lakes, I prefer an hour's drive from home. This is a loose guideline, but I generally need a spot close enough to be able to fish evenings and weekends.

Pressure Signs. Though in theory most secluded waters sustain little or no pressure, your first order of business at a new prospect site should be to assess the signs of use. Take a good look around at the landscape. Does it appear pristine, or is there evidence that others might frequent the location? Here's my rule of thumb: The degree of land impact directly correlates with the degree of impact on the fish population. To be brutally honest, I find that anglers tend to be the least "green" of outdoor sports and recreation folks. Hikers, horsemen, runners, and even mountain bikers leave a much smaller footprint than we do, particularly near water. The most prevalent trash items found near ponds and lakes include packaging from bait and tackle, beer cans, cigarettes, bobbers hanging from trees, and even toilet paper. That's all left behind by us.

If you see enough of it, or it appears to have been left recently, I advise moving on. On the other hand, if refuse is minimal and aged, you're probably OK. Tip: Keep plastic bags on hand and pick up as much trash as you can. This will allow you to monitor the area and determine whether it is getting new traffic. In general, anyone who visits the site and is careful not to leave anything behind is usually of no concern. Recall the correlation between land impact and fish impact: Those who take care of their surroundings will tend to do the same in the water. And if another fisher frequents this spot and takes care of it as you would, it's likely he's not harming fish or sharing information about the location either.

These are my own criteria on the parameters, but I am not suggesting that you develop rigid standards for your own site selection. Some of the best water may be just outside one of your parameters, so leave yourself enough wiggle room to discover it.

Legwork

The following are a few tips on making the best use of your time while being smart about safety.

Reconnaissance Missions. Those who fish in moving water will be able to relate to this advice. Many first trips to a new location involve more route-finding than fishing. The most common rookie mistake is underestimating everything—distance, time, and ease in following directions. I have spent off-season or winter days solely for route-finding, sometimes taking no fishing gear along. The lake I visit may even be frozen over at the time. Call it hiking with a purpose. The payoff is knowledge of exactly what to expect in the way of logistics when prime conditions arrive. This will afford not just the opportunity to maximize fishing time but also the ability to fish two or three prospects in a single day. For example, say you fish three ponds on a certain day and hit the jackpot on one of them. Because of your recon missions, you've likely done it much more quickly and efficiently than if you'd had to make two or three trips to one prospect just to find out whether it were viable. Recon also spares you from spending a 55-degree water day lost on a hillside somewhere, while a family of 17-inch cutts gets fat on emerging *Callibaetis* a half-mile away.

Another recon option is to leave the float tube and fly gear at home and just take a spinning rod with you. Often I'll throw a retractable into a day-pack with a few spoons and call it good. Now you're traveling light and spending much less time with "stuff" on a day when time is best spent on the move and covering water. Many sites will have shorelines that don't allow for a backcast anyway, and a day of roll casting while trying to determine the quality of a new pond falls short of smart. In good conditions, spoons worked over cover from shore are deadly, and I've never had a problem finding out what swims in a new lake this way.

I've even done this kind of research while mountain biking or trail running, and it has paid off. Several years ago I ran to the top of a ridge with a telescoping rod cinched to my Camel Pak. The pond up there was already familiar to me, but I hadn't fished it in some time. It was February, but the weather had been unseasonably warm that week—jackpot. I had no intention of staying long, just enough to get a feel for the place; and maybe I'd come back later with float tube and fly rod. Three hours—and 33 good-sized cutts—later, the fun began turning to guilt, so I finally quit and ran back down. Surprises like this do happen.

Beyond its usefulness as a recon tool, spin gear is every bit as legitimate as fly gear. It's all fishing, and you're simply taking advantage of the various tools available to you. A good angler is just that, regardless of the tools in his hands. He simply understands the order of priorities and lives by them: Find the right lake, find the fish in that lake, go after them with skilled hands, and the rest won't matter. Often the best fly fishers began as spin fishers. This type of fishing is a great tradition, and I still own all my spin gear. I use it proudly, and it makes me a better fly fisher.

Access and Logistics. Even secluded lakes and ponds tend to have a degree of ready access by trail. Other very worthwhile holes can be found off the beaten path, requiring a little scrambling or trail punching. Examples of trail punching might include reopening an existing legal trail that has grown over from lack of use, or beating back a few bushes as part of a scramble. In any case, no rules are being broken and you're not permanently altering the landscape (e.g., cutting live trees). In all circumstances, make sure you are aware of who owns the land and how it is sanctioned. If you're not 100-percent sure that your method to obtain access is allowed, wait and find out. Any access that requires trespassing or bending of the law is not an option.

The same cautions apply with respect to the lake itself. Make sure it is legal to fish, and be aware of seasonal or other restrictions. For example, seasonal limitations are usually in force for beaver ponds. Access restrictions may take some time to work through, but they can also serve as an effective barrier that keeps a good pond out of general reach.

A lightly traveled path through a wooded area marks the way to another secret haunt. Often these obscure routes lead to some very good surprises in terms of water with little to no pressure on the fish population.

Gaining access is often only the first of several challenges you may encounter. The second is usually put-in and takeout, since secluded lakes do not have amenities. Often your best choice for an entry and exit point will be the one with the fewest problems, though it's anything but perfect. Spend some time determining your spot, and always consider how well your prospective entry point allows you to get back out. Be aware of the surrounding structure, and never assume the bottom is really the bottom; most times when I plant my foot in a pond, I sink past my ankle into silt or mud. Again, slow down and take your time. You may be in a shallow spot, but getting wet won't enhance your angling experience—and if pond water has a smell, it's usually not a good one. Once afloat keep an eye out for at least one alternative point of exit. Sometimes what may have looked like a good choice at put-in will prove otherwise when it's time to hit dry land.

Safety and Security. The usual safety rules apply to fishing as to all outdoor activity: extra time, extra food, extra water, extra precaution. If you're brand-new to fly fishing in secluded spots, I also highly recommend the buddy system—at least at first. Cellphone, always. I also caution that

An open rock face with gradual slope like this is a rare find when it comes to secluded water. In most cases, time spent locating the best access is well worth it.

Just one of the rewards offered by secluded water, this brookie was surprisingly large at 14 inches. The respective pond covered only 2 acres.

whatever you have pictured from your map or set of directions is never a good representation of reality. Sometimes, once you get to your location, it can seem as if your map was for some other place in some other state: Other roads and trails not mapped, your route not visible, inaccurate distances, gated roads, washouts, and endless other surprises all add to the confusion. Expect confusion (and frustration), and expect to get lost now and then. Be careful to track distance and time elapsed on each road and trail you travel, and have a plan for retracing your steps. The only thing worse than not finding the lake you were looking for is not finding your way back. Also be alert to the passage of time and the hour of nightfall.

Fishing secluded water often involves leaving your rig at a trailhead. My own rig has been a target for theft more than once; on one occasion I even heard the entire assault, as I sat on the edge of a mountain lake while my car was being broken into a half-mile up the hill. Spend any amount of time outdoors and you'll have stories of your own to tell. Cardinal rule: No valuables left in your rig. Insurance can cover any extensive vehicle damage.

Prime fishing can be had at this end of the pond, but not today. The new family here will remain undisturbed.

To this point, I've outlined the basic method of finding lakes, reservoirs, and ponds that offer good or exceptional fishing. What else?

Take Good Care of It. I would strongly encourage any angler to protect small water habitats and their surrounding land and wildlife as much as possible. Pack out any debris, including discarded leader and tippet materials. I usually go a step further and pick up anything left behind by those who came before me. You can't always get it all, but leaving a place cleaner than when you arrived certainly doesn't hurt. And if you need to "use the woods," leave no visible trace.

With respect to wildlife, I limit my own interaction to taking a few photos. Obviously don't feed the animals, and keep your distance from identifiable habitat, particularly areas with eggs or offspring. I myself will avoid whole sections of lakes where creatures are nesting. Whether you are aware of it or not, getting too close to them stresses wildlife. A couple of extra fish are never worth it.

Resources. I avoid reading books that tell you to "fish here." I know there are also plenty of local fly-fishing guidebooks that will tell you where to find the blue ribbon water. I want to emphasize that the places listed in these resources are not the types of lakes and ponds that this book refers to. Instead, my approach is to encourage you to seek out the undiscovered for yourself. These places exist; I wouldn't be out there if they didn't. There are certainly many well-written local guidebooks; however, I'm simply describing a different experience, one that I believe many fly fishers are looking for.

Find a state atlas, and keep it in your rig when you're not studying it in your living room. Probably every angler I know owns one, and for good reason. A state atlas is the best basic reference for mapped roads, trails, and water. However, I would not recommend relying on the atlas for specific hiking trail information; it just doesn't drill down that far. I have a small handful of local trail guides, and these tend to provide very good detail on route finding, elevation, expected timing, and so on. Depending on your search area, the major online aerial photo sites can be highly useful at times, particularly for forest service roads and getting a first glance at the terrain. I've also surfed these web sites to seek out new water in an area and have had several successes.

I also rely heavily on my state fishing guide for general information. These guides are very simple and well-designed books that receive updates every few years. I find them reasonably accurate and highly useful. They are great for basics such as species information, acreage, elevation, and directions. I don't rely on them for "best fishing" information, though; that's our job.

Lastly, you'll want to use your state stocking reports to get an idea of what swims where. Remember the tip about looking for small stocking numbers. I would also recommend extending your research into stocking numbers over a period of several seasons; five years is about right. Over time, you'll develop a good sense about what to expect in the water based on those reports. As you gain experience in interpreting information and relating it to specific bodies of water, you'll discover that a surprising number of larger fish is out there waiting to be caught. The information is there; you just never hear about it. And to follow that thought . . .

About Secrets. They're not a bad thing. When it's someone else's treasured fishing spot, never ask them to give it up. If a friend wants you to know about it, he'll offer. If he does, always respect his valuable information by protecting it. He shouldn't have to ask you to keep it to yourself. When someone gives you information, it means they trust you. Offer some assurance that you'll die with the knowledge undisclosed—right after you express some appreciation for the trust afforded. In my opinion, the trust of a friend is more valuable than some honey hole will ever be.

When the secret location is yours, think seriously about whom you share it with. If you feel you need to ask someone not to reveal your information, you're sharing it with the wrong person. I share with trusted friends only, and I've never once asked them to keep quiet. I don't need to.

If you ask me, information sharing should go both ways between anglers. It should be a way of extending appreciation for good friends. However, if it's the primary means by which you find water and fish, something is wrong.

About Fishing Reports. By now you probably know what I'm going to say: If this is the primary way you find water, something is wrong. Whether you're at the fly shop, the boat launch, or hanging out online, a good rule of thumb is to give them out more often than using them. A report is no better than day-old news. It's a starting point at best, but 99 percent of success in burying the hook will still come from your own puzzle-solving skills. I'd suggest that if you run across reports of old honey holes, there's a reason that information is now available: That red hot pond or section of skinny water that wouldn't quit back in '78 doesn't hold those fish anymore. A lot can happen over time, and the only thing constant about water is change. Unless you have information from within the last year or so, someone's old haunts from back in the day are worthless—or at least have no better odds of success than anyplace else. Recent information is king.

If you're looking for specific information about a place, using the search function in a local online forum—just to see who knows what—is worth doing. I wouldn't expect anything outright, but you'd be surprised at how much a lot of anglers are willing to share. Many are quite passionate about the sport and are generally glad to help out. Online relationships are the same as face-to-face: a little respect and appreciation go a long way. Along the same lines, developing a network of friends here and on the water certainly never hurts.

For my money, water earned is the sweetest there is. No handouts or charity, it's yours. If you ask me, the entire art of fishing is defined by one's ability to track down and lure fish successfully. To me, this means the entire process. When someone else tells you where to find a fish, who really caught it?

Finally, think of all the secluded lakes and ponds you've ever run across: Maybe you were hiking; perhaps you've even tried fishing one or

Some secrets are worth keeping when it comes to small lakes and ponds. I don't visit this one often enough, but it never disappoints.

two of them. You may even know of one that you've never considered exploring with rod and reel. Fishing waters are famous for keeping secrets, particularly about their inhabitants. *Surely*, you may be thinking, *a population of fish could not sustain in such a small and shallow body of water. And even if it could, what are the odds of anything sizable?* And so begins the deception.

Thinking a population of trout cannot survive, or would have nowhere to run or hide in a cramped environment, is the usual start of an angler's downfall when it comes to these hidden spots. Soon enough, he concludes the place is barren and moves on to other, more promising, lowland waters where the trout are anything but a secret. Yes, these trout may leave a little to be desired in terms of size and smarts, but they are so easily and conveniently taken. Besides, you can drive right up and jump right in. Maybe sharing the lake with everyone else, along with a little noise and some litter here and there, isn't so bad.

For many fly fishers, the notion of something that feels like work is enough to deter them. But for those who decide the rewards are worth it, angling in secluded waters, discovered through our own efforts, offers the stuff we all want but can't seem to find at that easily accessible lake up the road. And if the itch for adventure has led you out there in search of a good secret, remember there's a lot more going on beneath the surface than you realize. If you assume up front that trout can live just about anywhere, while deceiving predators like you with behavior that hides their existence, you're on the right track. Give your find a solid chance by fishing it more than once, and spending some real time there, especially if you have positive stocking reports. Again, these places tend to be productive on their own unique schedules; and in my experience, you won't necessarily hit the jackpot on your first try.

Lesson 2

LOCATING TROUT

What differentiates successful anglers from the rest is that they prioritize their tactics into the most effective order: WHEN–WHERE–HOW–WHAT. Ignoring that sequence is the fastest way to forego opportunity. Example: An angler arrives at the lake and decides on an Olive Bugger trolled slowly behind a floating line. Why? First, he's caught fish that way before; it's what he knows. Second, he can cover the entire lake this way, ensuring that the fish have nowhere to hide. And, of course, it's what everyone else on the lake is doing. Ten hours later, he's landed seven fish and feels rather satisfied.

The question I would ask is, is this the experience we want from stillwater fly fishing? For me, the better experience is at another lake, where a fisher has spent the same 10-hour period observing conditions, interpreting clues, solving the puzzle of WHEN and WHERE active fish are to be found, and enjoying the benefits. This lake may well have yielded 50 or more fish to our diligent angler. Even if it hasn't, the fly fisher in this case has been working hard, brain fully engaged, and executing well—instead of trolling around, hoping for the next lucky strike. (We will discuss the meaning of good execution later in the book.)

The preceding paragraph also raises an important reminder: Always know when to stop if you're experiencing success on the water. Continuous pressure, even by catch-and-release, can put unnecessary stress on a lake. I won't attempt a hard definition here given all the variables, but keep this issue in mind any time the action heats up. On lowland lakes, stress tends to be treated as less of an issue in light of more aggressive stocking, the often larger acreage of most waters, and the known pressures that come from high use. In these waters, the majority of plants are harvested quickly, general regulations are in force, and larger catches are an accepted practice. On smaller and more secluded lakes and ponds, I usually cap my take at 10—even 5, at times—as a rule of thumb.

And for what it's worth, you can't control your take at day's end—assuming you did your best and didn't stop on some arbitrary number. It just depends on the circumstances and available opportunities that day. Moreover, your own priorities will dictate the results you get. Let's face it, we each define fun a little differently, and if all this stuff we're discussing weren't fun for me, I'd fish differently or find a new sport. In that way, a guy might enjoy the day best with a 4-fish effort, another guy may find 30 more his speed, and still another doesn't really care and may get skunked and go home happier than the rest of us. How you spend your time on the water is never wrong, and doing things in a way that is far from productive is also never wrong. It's all just part of the learning process, and figuring out what doesn't work is half of it. By simply showing up, you've already won. This means there is a degree of subjectivity in how you and I define success and fulfillment on the water. The following will assist you in your efforts to locate and ultimately catch more fish; however, the endgame for each of us may involve more than simply landing every fish possible.

SOLVING THE PUZZLE

Imagine showing up for an outing you've been looking forward to. Now imagine the following: You look across the lake and see an endless sea of nothing. Just water. No rises. No bugs. No swallows skimming the surface for an easy meal. Nothing. Then maybe you get in and fish for an hour. Two hours. Again, nothing. Sound familiar?

It may seem as if you have brought everything you would need for a successful day at the lake—pontoon, rod and reel, spare spool with sinker, fly box, net; you even remembered the oars this time. The list goes on, until your rig won't fit a whole lot more, so surely you didn't forget anything important. Or did you?

May I suggest three things more valuable than anything on your list: some general knowledge about conditions, a plan based on that knowledge, and a bit of confidence. Confidence, in particular.

Of course, we also don't need to limit this to three; but those are essential for taking the lake scenario we just described and turning it into a successful outing. Other useful tools might include the information from my last trip to the lake—assuming it was recent—and a fishing report. While I am against using reports as the only way to find water and fish, I acknowledge that a report can be useful if the information is recent, reliable, and reasonably written. A good fishing report can be a useful addition to your toolbox; you just don't want it to *be* your toolbox.

Before we look at conditions, a word about predictability. No matter how good you get at interpreting all the clues in a given day, solving the puzzle is never 100 percent science. I'd love to be able to tell you that, if we follow a certain set of rules, we can constantly be on fish. And, if you're skilled and diligent, you *can* get yourself a lot closer to that ideal on a regular basis. However, fishing will always include unpredictable elements that defy logic.

I consider this sport to be about 80 percent skill and experience and the other 20 percent a simple roll of the dice. That's fishing. Now, that 80 percent goes a long way toward determining frequent success on the water. If

Unfortunately, not everything is explainable when it comes to trout behavior, but you can still enjoy the results of good observation and execution without having a full understanding. This cutthroat was a willing taker in direct sunlight out and away from any cover. No visible food sources were present to explain its location and behavior either, so I did what any angler should for lack of an explanation—I went looking for more.

you're experienced, you'll tend to do well every time out, but there will always be a piece of the puzzle you can't make fit—and sometimes it's a very big piece. The good news is you can still make use of it. Whenever something I can't explain occurs, I accept it, observe the consequences, and learn from it. I may or may not figure out precisely what's happening, but if I can recognize one of these occurrences when it repeats in the future, I may be able to profit from it without ever fully understanding it.

Fly fishers enjoy or even prefer stillwater for a number of reasons: convenience, sometimes larger fish, beautiful scenery, relaxation, good alternative when the rivers are blown, and so on. I have several of my own reasons, but one in particular would be enough for me: I'm in it for the puzzle, and it's a new and different puzzle each time, with no two ever alike.

Weather Conditions

For me, fishing begins well before the actual outing. I start looking at weather conditions as much as a week ahead of time. The forecast rarely determines my decision to go, but it does serve as a starting point for my plan. What I'm looking for is the degree to which temperatures and other weather conditions are predicted to be close to, or far from, ideal on the day of the outing. Of course, weather alone is not a reliable predictor of fish activity; it is simply one factor within the much larger, more complex picture.

Again, optimum water temperature for trout activity is somewhere in the neighborhood of 55 degrees F. By studying recent weather conditions, you can usually make a pretty good guess about lake conditions. With some experience, you'll be able to predict lag times from outside air to water, and to know when a change will affect activity for better or worse. Let's break some of that down.

The Four Seasons

You can begin predicting how conditions will affect your next outing simply by considering the time of year. In general spring and fall tend to be best, summer presents a few challenges but is usually fishable, and winter brings the greatest limitations. This is not to suggest that, say, the month of April always offers outstanding fishing. Rather, it's a matter of correlation. Spring and fall are highly correlated with mild weather conditions that result in ideal water temperatures. Warmer summer days heat up lakes and ponds and make fish less energetic. Winter cools the water, with similar effects on fish activity. In addition, winter may mean frozen water in many areas, putting fly fishing on hiatus until spring thaw.

The point here is that making assumptions about seasons and good fishing is not enough. You'll want to look beyond the time of year and focus on recent weather trends. I previously mentioned an unseasonably warm February when the fish went on a feeding frenzy. Sometimes we may get a stubborn March that holds spring activity off for an extra month. So after considering how the time of year "should" affect fishing conditions, you'll want to research whether conditions are typical of the current month or not. Again, the further you go from 55-degree water in either direction, the less optimum the conditions are for fish activity.

Lag Times

Assume it's midsummer and the last two weeks saw daytime highs above 80 degrees F. A significant cooling trend starts Thursday, with a drop of perhaps 20 degrees in some places. Will the water at your lake be cooler by the weekend? Individual lakes warm up and cool down at different rates, but in general, most lakes cannot fully react to temperature change in two days' time. It's not an exact science, but with enough observation, you can begin estimating lag times between weather events and their effect on water conditions.

If you live near waters that ice over in the winter, you can observe their freezing and thawing pattern as a learning tool. As temperatures drop, record how long it takes different bodies of water to freeze over, noting the difference between larger and smaller lakes and ponds. Then, in the spring, record the thawing patterns. Note the temperature trends that produce the thaw. This is a good exercise, and those observation skills can be adapted and applied to any part of the year. Lag times vary, and it's useful to learn how they work in your favorite waters.

Gradual versus Severe Change

This is a big one. Any time a new weather system arrives with a change in temperature, the rate of that change will have a direct impact on trout activity. I've observed that steep rates of temperature change significantly affect trout behavior, whereas gradual rates tend not to as much. This makes sense: To a degree, rapid change invariably throws the system into shock, thus causing a sharp decline in activity. This means fish simply lay low after a hard change of any kind, coming back gradually over a period of several days or longer—*gradually* being the key word. This is why you hear so many anglers talking about the importance of stable weather. On the other hand, I wouldn't assume that an overnight change would throw the fish into shock, because a fast approaching new system might have little or no effect on water temperature. In short, water temperature is the primary driver of activity (among conditions), and you'll want to watch the rate and degree of any change.

The Depths

When temperatures change rapidly or are less than optimum, fish tend to locate and hold in deeper water—escaping the more severe fluctuations in the surface and shallow layers—while they adjust to conditions. When I talk about deeper water, I am referring to depths of 10 to 25 feet. Below that range, light, food supplies, and oxygen diminish to the point that fish have little reason to venture there. And while their activity level usually drops when they move to deeper water, fish don't "fall asleep" or quit feeding altogether.

When the trout population moves to deeper waters, you'll want to take your presentation there as well. Most anglers agree that a slower presentation is best in this circumstance; however don't assume that a deep fish is also a lethargic one. Try to understand why the fish is down there in the first place. If the reason is to avoid a greater degree of shock from surface temperatures, that's one thing. If the fish is in deeper water to chase down a major food source, you would expect a different level of activity. Then again, a group of fish may be holding at a depth where food is scarce, and competition is stiff for the next small fuzzy thing that comes swimming along. In that case, your speedy presentation might provoke a determined strike. The fact is, you can't always know the precise reason fish are holding deep, so don't rule out experimenting with different approaches.

Warm Weather

In typical summer weather, I tend to look for most action early and late in the day (late is usually better), but I am not offering this as a hard-and-fast rule. Cooler temperatures and lower light are the primary reasons I expect early and late fish activity, but I always consider the food sources as well. A strong damsel hatch that goes, say, from noon to 4 p.m., will bring a good part of the fish population to the table. Feeding may last for most of that period, regardless of warmer surface temperatures—especially if that's the most substantial food source of the day.

Is there such a thing as being too hot to fish? Absolutely yes—and my response is based on concern for the health and well-being of the fish. Generally, surface temperatures around 70 degrees are considered the cutoff. There is no *absolute* cutoff, but if you are concerned about the surface temperature or fish behavior, or feeling a little guilty about continuing, it's time to get off the water.

Also remember that you can use a deeper presentation. Often, though not always, a fly worked further down will produce surprisingly well during the day.

Cold Weather
In milder climates, where ice is less of a factor, those deeper water layers will still offer some insulation from the biting chill near surface. In these regions, the warmth of midday will often bring fish up for a time. I never

A nice brown taken against shore in cold weather. Low light at dusk brought the fish shallow in search of food, while a Bullet-Head Minnow presented swiftly near the film drew it without hesitation.

rule out any part of the day for fishing in winter, nor do I neglect the shallower layers when looking for fish. Nevertheless, I generally start with the depths and a slower presentation, and go from there. Is there such a thing as it being too cold to fish? Personally, I consider it too cold only when the lake is frozen over. Coldwater fishing offers more than enough opportunity for an experienced angler; however, those less experienced, less motivated, or less tolerant of the cold may have a different opinion. If winter fishing isn't fun for you, by all means don't waste your time. Go skiing and come back in the spring.

Mild Weather

OK, so it's early May or perhaps mid-November, and conditions couldn't be better. Weather has been stable, temperatures are ideal, there are signs of food everywhere, and fish can be found all over the place. Well, there may be no issue catching fish; however, we're back to that seven-fish-versus-fifty thing. When it's ripe, the game becomes one of capitalizing. Arrive early, stay late, and fish for all you're worth in between.

Rain

Often this falls under the "just right" category. If you don't mind the rain, get out and fish in it (short of storm conditions). Some of my best fishing days have been in the rain or just after it—not always, but most of the time. Any time the weather can reduce surface visibility it works to an angler's advantage. Trout tend to be less bashful about feeding when they aren't as easily spotted. I'm referring to surface conditions here—not about mud and murky water. At the very least, I'd factor rain in on the positive side unless it becomes excessive. My advice: Invest in good rain gear and learn to love it.

More on visibility: Perhaps a few extra words here would help, since much of what I do on the water is governed by visibility. With one or two exceptions, weather conditions and time of day largely determine water and surface visibility. Most of what I encounter—and am concerned with—has to do more with surface visibility than with water clarity. Surface visibility is probably the one major factor that can turn fish behavior on a dime, sometimes faster than food. Often—even multiple times during an outing—surface visibility will change in an instant, and either curtail or bring on the action.

Attempting to describe each situation and its effect is probably futile; the best thing you can do is constantly pay attention to what's going on

Running for cover. Once hooked, a fish is just as likely to run straight down, or even toward you, as it is to run out and away. Instinctively, it makes more sense for the fish to prioritize finding cover over getting away from the angler at the other end of the line. In fact, don't be surprised if your next fish decides to use you as its chosen hiding place. On many occasions, I've chased them out from underneath my own float tube.

with surface visibility and factor it into your decisions throughout the day. Visibility of food certainly matters, but I think the greatest impact comes from focusing on how visible the fish themselves are, both to their predators and to some of their prey. Instinctively, fish are quite tuned-in to their own camouflage at any moment—and every time they contemplate a meal, that issue is considered first. They simply can't afford not to. So the way you and I can break all that down is by lighting and cover. I'll make a big generalization here, but it works. Generally, less light equals less visibility equals more activity. And generally, more cover equals less visibility equals more activity.

I think of cover in terms of two things: surface chop and structure. Surface chop is just the degree to which the lake surface is roughed up by the wind. Watch for sudden changes in feeding behavior every time the surface changes. It doesn't happen every time, but it happens enough to warrant attention. Structure can be any one of a hundred things that fish may use to hide: docks, bridges, boats, tree-overhang, fallen trees, stumps, rocks, you name it. Interestingly, I've had countless fish, once hooked, try to use me as structure to take refuge. Some have run straight into my lap when I was in a float tube. Structure is not weather-related, but it can still have a lot to do with visibility. More on fishing structure later; for now just think of it as anyplace where fish often locate.

To summarize, trout behavior and activity are largely influenced by the conditions at hand. It follows that much of your success will be largely determined by your ability to observe and interpret weather trends, rates of temperature change, and other influences, and then make informed decisions based on that combination of factors. Just be sure you realize that, despite all these factors and how much we may know about them, we're still trying to predict the behavior of an unpredictable creature. True, you can get pretty good at it, but with trout anything can happen. Nothing is a sure bet, of course, but a good working knowledge of conditions as they relate to trout behavior will up your odds considerably, along with your results.

My next advice would be to find a thermometer and measure surface temperatures whenever you go out. Note that temperatures are different throughout the depths. Still, you can get a lot of useful data just by tracking the surface and relating it to the outside air, on one end, and fish activity, on the other.

Food

Now onto the other big one: food. Here we'll hit the handful of insects and other organisms with the greatest significance as trout food in a stillwater environment. The good news is, you don't need a formal degree to understand how trout are likely to feed, and how you can take advantage of their patterns. Fly fishers should at least recognize the major ones—that handful of food sources that occur most frequently on lakes and make up the majority of a trout's diet.

The following is a list of the major trout foods typically found in lakes. With each, I'll identify general timing of hatches and some basic characteristics, and then offer a few tips on burying the hook.

Mayflies (*spring/early summer/fall*). In nymph form, they may last several months or longer, staying near the lake bottom among plant life. When hatched, they take on functional wings but will still moult (or shed) one

Adult *Callibaetis*. One of the most common mayfly species in western lakes, the *Callibaetis* can hatch in prolific numbers in concentrated areas along a lake's shallows. Look for some of the best dry-fly opportunities of the year when they pop at surface. A good hatch can last over two hours, usually around midday, and the cycle can go on for several weeks during spring.

additional time before becoming a full adult. In that middle stage, the mayfly is known among fly anglers as a "dun," and the full adult as a "spinner." Duns may live a few hours or less, and spinners share the same short lifespan. In general appearance, adults have long curved bodies, forked tails, and large upright wings.

Callibaetis, *Hexagenia*, *Siphlonurus*, and *Tricorythodes* are good stillwater examples, with *Callibaetis* generally the most common. I'll use *Callibaetis* as the example here, since they are the most widespread. Typically, they range in hook size from #12 in spring, down to #16 later in the year. In spring, hatches can be prolific, lasting one to two hours or more each day and continuing for up to several weeks. *Callibaetis* can be a lake's primary food source at times, resulting in fish feeding very little, or not at all, when the hatch is off. I've seen days when the only time worth showing up was during the hatch, but the action can be the best of the year on dry flies. At other times, midges will run in unison, making for exceptionally productive days for anglers. Watch for *Callibaetis* hatches to occur at slightly different times each day and to last for varying duration, depending on conditions. Before the *Callibaetis* emerge, I generally fish nymphs for an hour or so prior to the time when I think they'll come up. Good for a few strikes, and useful as a gauge for upcoming surface action—but I find the numbers tend to happen once the hatches hit surface and fish are rising. To be in the middle of it is truly one of the highlights of the year, as even the lake's largest inhabitants will show up hungry.

Look for the action over shoals (shallow areas) with vegetation along the bottom, and remember to give it that short hesitation on hook sets in all

The warm sun hitting my sleeve creates prime real estate for this mayfly. Timing their hatches during spring is a worthwhile effort that can yield good results with a floating presentation.

the excitement. An emerger is my usual weapon of choice. They attract fish nicely in this circumstance, and the lower hanging hook point tends to grab and hold even better with these aggressive takes. Keep a fair number of them on hand. Tip: Swallows tend to go hand in hand with these hatches, and are just as gullible as fish when it comes to your fly. They'll try to pick it up, but they practically never stick to it. A second or two and they'll drop it. Though I find it annoying, I just leave them alone and deal with it. Small price to pay for action this good.

While we're on the subject of swallows, if you ever snag or tangle one while casting, I find it best to gently bring them to the net and very carefully get the hook away. At that point they get very timid, so you shouldn't get much resistance. Make sure the bird is completely free of your line before attempting to let it go. I learned that the hard way my first time, and watched as one still wrestling with a short length of my tippet became eagle food. Since then I've had a perfect record.

Caddis/Trichoptera (*late spring/early summer*). One of the more popular general-purpose stillwater drys, the Elk Hair Caddis (EHC) makes a great utility fly. They work well in the evening when takes are more than a sip. In terms of matching them on the water, I identify these as the moth-like ones. Development goes from larva to pupa within a self-constructed shell that is affixed to underwater structure. Then the mature pupa cuts it way out, swims to the surface to shed its skin, and emerges as a full-on adult. Adults usually live between one and two weeks. Trout will feed on them in all stages of the caddis's life.

Caddisflies are also called sedges. Cinnamon Sedges, Traveling Sedges, and Rush Sedges are three examples of common species known to inhabit stillwater. Look for them to emerge in shallow vegetation near shore. Size generally ranges from #8 to #14, and for subsurface presentation, anglers would do well to present a slow imitation via Type 1 or 2 full sink, or a floater with long-enough leader (a sinking tip would also work here). When working the shallows, remember to position yourself out and away from your targeted area, and pay attention to things like surface visibility and any signs of fish moving in the area. One other tip: On a missed strike, try leaving your fly in place instead of pulling out right away to recast. Often, you stand better odds of a comeback if the fly remains where it was missed—particularly in highly visible shallows where trout are already more cautious.

For dry-fly presentation, be sure to limit the number of casts you make. (Too many, or too often, is too much when it comes to the shallows.) Also, keep reminding yourself to allow that hesitation before any hook set. And

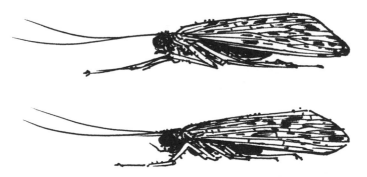

Caddisfly (Sedge). Similar to moths in appearance, adults are often found around shallow vegetation near the shoreline. Common stillwater examples include the Cinnamon Sedge (top), known for its evening activity, and Traveling Sedge (bottom), which has a more rounded wing tip and is known for its tendency to run, or skate, across the lake surface.

again, if a standard dry just isn't sticking to anything, give a lower-hanging emerger a shot.

Chironomidae (*year-round, with hatches spring/summer/fall*). Part of the midge family, Chironomidae are a nonbiting version, thankfully. On one occasion, I had the pleasure of encountering their biting cousins overseas; I won't be first in line to experience that again. Adults are similar in size and appearance to mosquitoes, larvae look like short segmented worms, and pupa will develop a small white puff near the head. At each stage, Chironomidae can be any one of several colors. A bright-red version of the larva (bloodworm) is one example popular among fly fishers. Adults mate in flight; then they usually lay their eggs along the lake surface. The eggs hatch into larva that form in the mud along the lake floor (although some species are free-swimming). Larvae then develop into the pupa stage before making their way to the surface to emerge. Breaking the surface and emerging usually takes less than a minute before the adult is ready to fly off. Adults may live only a few hours or up to several weeks before they mate and die off.

If you ask me, Chironomidae are the quintessential lake food. They tend to occur anytime and anywhere, yet I rarely look to match them. One simple reason: I have good success using other presentations that don't exactly imitate. Really it's a matter of preference—and with Chironomidae activity, you can often get away with it, especially at depth. That said, Chi-

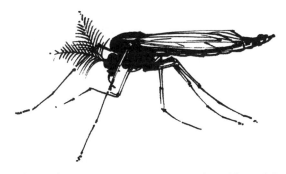

Adult midge. Similar to the mosquito in appearance, the midge adult can vary widely in size, even within a single body of water. Although they can provide decent dry-fly action, don't expect the same intensity or opportunity as with mayflies. Midges can be more widespread than mayflies, both in terms of timing and location, and they tend to provide a lot of subsurface or deepwater action, where Chironomids (midge larvae) may be present in large numbers.

Newly hatched midge adult.

ronomid imitation is a very common and legitimate form of stillwater fly fishing, and I always appreciate the anglers who do it religiously and execute well. There is an art to it beyond sitting around staring at a bobber. (We'll take an introductory look at Chironomid fishing in the next lesson).

Since a midge hatch can be fished effectively either by direct imitation or other means, I usually present a leech or other common lake pattern once I dial the depth in. As long as I know they're down there, I can almost always make it work. Sometimes I out-fish the Chironomid anglers, sometimes not. But when a guy is good at it and has the feed pegged, it can be rather tough outdoing numbers like that. Still, the same or better results can be produced in other circumstances by other methods. That means using a Chironomid is far from the only way to hit fish after fish during a midge hatch. It can happen in lots of other ways. Obviously the biggest take goes to the fisher who is proficient at both methods.

What to look for: Sometimes, rolling trout are the big tip-off, but that's a fraction of the time at best. Besides visible midges peppered across the lake surface, watch for the abundance of shucks left behind. They tend to be a half-inch long or a little smaller. Another great way of spotting a midge hatch is when swallows are present. If the birds appear to be feeding off the surface, you can usually get in close and observe them picking off bugs as they first take flight. A rather interesting drill is to watch the bugs as they

Empty Chironomid shuck.

break free, and observe how fast they get snatched up. Often it's well under 10 seconds when swallows are really active.

Learning Chironomid hatch cycles—along with observing the relative amount of activity on the lake surface—can tip the angler off to the timing of unseen trout activity below.

Seeing the invisible (Chironomidae at depth): Worth knowing—there are times when Chironomid activity and feeding trout can go undetected until it's too late. For that reason, I highly recommend getting familiar with hatch cycles where you fish. Case in point: On a recent fall outing, the bite had been slow all morning, with little to speak of through midday. The weather was clear and unseasonably warm, the usual makings of a dead afternoon. The lake had seen recent midges at sporadic times, but it was occasional at best. In fact, I had been out the prior day in foul weather when there was no midge activity to speak of; the bite came on hard that evening when minnows thickened up, and that's when most trout were taken. But the next day's change to mild conditions had me wondering if Chironomidae would liven up and affect the bite.

On that hunch, I began searching the depths at an outer shoal where activity typically took place. Sure enough, about lunchtime it got started. The strikes came slowly at first. Then the action picked up over the next hour and a half, and I managed a run of eleven fish before things cooled off. Interestingly, by then the first signs of the hatch were just beginning to show at surface. Before then, nothing was emerging visibly, no empty shucks could be spotted, and even the swallows were nowhere to be found.

So, in this example, by the time there were visible clues of midge activity, feeding among trout had largely run its course. Tough as that is, an angler can still capitalize in one of two ways: either by knowing the trend as described here, or by accident and recognition (i.e., you encounter a few strikes by coincidence, make some observations, and interpret them correctly). It's not uncommon for trout to feed deeper down like this, particularly if surface temperature or visibility are uncomfortable for them. In this case, it could have been something like that—or after a couple hours of feeding, the fish simply may have been full by the time of emergence. A final observation, and no surprise: On that second day, when midges were active, the bite was far less intense on minnows that evening than on the first day, when trout hadn't been feeding beforehand.

Dragonflies (*summer*). In nymph form, they make an attractive meal for trout; in adult form dragonflies are a less common food, given their size and behavior. You'll see them taking flight on calm summer days. As a pattern, the dragonfly nymph is a sizable fly good for trolling and general searching. Near the lake floor, along any shoal, is a good bet.

Dragonfly adult. Opportunities may be limited in terms of perfecting a direct imitation; however, in nymph form, the dragonfly shines as a general stillwater search pattern.

Damsels (*late spring/all summer*). The dragonfly's little blue cousin. These are more populous than dragonflies and generally abundant on warm summer afternoons. Fortunately, they don't have annoying habits when swarms occur. At most, they may look to you for a temporary place to land, but I haven't found that to be a problem. Conversely, I'm rather entertained at holding out my hand as a landing pad—and their willingness to accept the invitation. They'll usually sit and mind themselves if left undisturbed.

I find when damsels start to show in numbers, usually late morning or early afternoon, fish will be found chasing the nymphs as they make a run for shore. In general, a damsel nymph lives among vegetation and then swims up toward shore at hatch time. There, it may climb out onto a stem or structure that extends above the surface. Adults live for several weeks or longer, depending on time of development.

The textbook method of presenting suggests placing yourself right against shore, casting outward, and retrieving back. However, staying outward, casting inward, and retrieving back yields the same result in my experience. Logically, I don't ever like placing my body right up against shore, where fish may be located in a foot of water. Besides, the cast outward can

Easily recognizable, damsels are generally long and slender, with bright blue coloring. They can show in good numbers during a hatch, often grouped along the shoreline. When this occurs, an angler is smart to zero in and get to work in the immediate area. Rest assured the lake's trout population won't let them go to waste.

be less than convenient. The other rule I often break is imitation, in that I may not use an actual damsel pattern. A mini-leech works just fine, as do a number of other patterns with the same general size and appearance. A final note: Nearly all feeding on damsels occurs when they are in nymph form, so I don't recommend much—or any—use of the adult version as a dry fly. In fact, when feeding on nymphs has been prolific against shore, I've had much better success on a small emerger if I want to work the surface. Trout will gladly take other forms of food when feeding on damsels, yet presenting an adult imitation is usually ineffective. Go figure.

Minnows (*year-round*). These make a hearty meal for all trout, lunkers in particular. I've had very good success working a minnow-infested shoal or shoreline—or blind searching with a minnow pattern in low light or darkness. Epoxy head patterns are as close to perfect as I have found, in terms of casting dynamics and appearance. Maybe it's just the right amount of epoxy. Whatever the reason, they do their job exceptionally well. I'm also not averse to using a deceiver or other saltwater pattern in certain circumstances (large browns, assertive feeding, etc.). This can be one of those times when a hard, aggressive approach and fast retrieve are effective and a lot of fun.

Minnows can concentrate in any shallow area or along the shoreline, at any part of the day. A good minnow feed can be a lot like *Callibaetis*, in that your heavy-hitters will all show up for the meal. Keep in mind that the best action is not necessarily right up in that visibly-concentrated zone against shore, especially once the feed has been there a while. Too often, I've seen anglers pull right up against, or on top of, this feeding area and wonder why so many visible fish won't have anything to do with their fly. Or, at best, they'll manage one or two fish and then waste a good hour sitting there, continuing to make the same cast. Truth is, a good minnow feed will afford 10, even 20 or more fish to the net if you play it smart. The problem in-close is that the shallow area is highly visible, and fish will be more than cautious while feeding there. The other problem is you and your fake minnow are competing against thousands of real minnows in a very small amount of space. The point is that much of your action will likely be where the fish are not visible. Fine to make a few casts in tight, where you can see everything, but then move on as soon as you stop drawing strikes.

Two other places worth your attention: just off the edge of that shallow zone, where you no longer see what's going on; and the surrounding open water. That edge will hold some of your better fish, ones that lurk just off

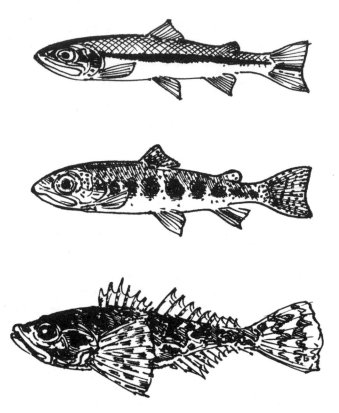

Within a lake, minnows, trout fry, and other small fish are prevalent food sources for larger trout. At times, these small fish can school up near vegetation or in the shallows, where hungry trout will often show up in numbers to partake. Pay attention at dusk or in other low lighting, when feeding trout will become more aggressive, even breaking the surface as they give chase.

the frenzy and lazily pick off anything that strays just out of the zone. Those fish are much more willing takers when it comes to your presentation. Then, out in the open water, you may or may not see minnows at the surface. Either way, I would suggest spending at least half of your time working out there. And practically no one does. That area will be alive with activity during a minnow feed; you just don't see it. You can work that outer area and diligently set the hook in one fish after the next, while others might squat on that little circle of visible feeding and get blanked.

If you remember nothing else about minnows, just note that often the best action can be had where you can't see what's going on beneath the surface.

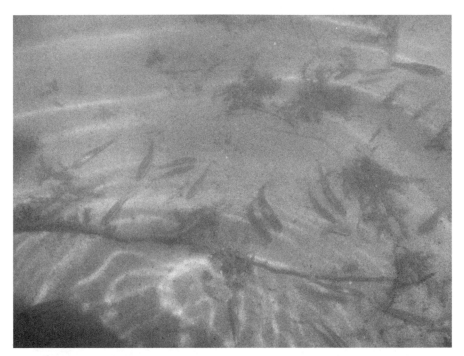

A school of minnows gathers in the shallows on a warm day in June. Even in the bright afternoon sun, this was enough food to call in good numbers of larger trout. Fishing was exceptional for several hours while these minnows were schooled up along shore.

In the absence of a minnow feed, a minnow pattern is still good for the shoreline in low light, or at any time during fall. A minnow is also a good general-purpose fly for searching open water or trolling.

Leeches (*year-round*). I have a hard time believing that these are a major part of a trout's diet in most lakes; however, I throw a mini-leech 95 percent of the time all year. It's not like leeches are found in grouped abundance like an insect hatch or minnow school—at least not where anglers are concerned. And if it does happen, I'd hate to be out for a swim in the middle of them.

I'm mentioning leeches here for the simple reason that I mimic them constantly when I know fish aren't actively out for them. But it has nothing to do with the actual imitation. In fact, I have no interest in making a leech pattern act like a leech in the water. I go strictly by current activity and behavior; if it's spring and I'm sitting in 46-degree water, I'll find fish and start ripping it around pretty fast. Those fish don't care in the least that my

Though prevalent in many of our western lakes, leeches are typically seen far less often by anglers than are other foods, since leeches tend to stay hidden. Even so, they make great trout food. As a fly pattern, the leech can be a highly effective utility fly for subsurface presentation, given its universal size and appearance.

fake fly doesn't swim and wiggle around like a leech should. All they see is this brown fuzzy thing in a panic, swimming for its life. The next thought that crosses their minds is swallowing it before another fish does and then on to the next.

What makes the leech such a good stillwater fly is its universal appearance, along with its ideal casting and handling dynamics with a sinking line. Moreover, it works—and it works well. Its size is right in the middle of what larger trout feed on, and, truth be told, a fish rarely holds out for one specific thing when on the hunt, even when working a hatch. In my experience, when fish are in feeding mode, they'll usually take anything edible if presented well. Of course, there are exceptions to everything. For instance, if trout all around you are rising to a major *Callibaetis* hatch, it's time to put away the sinking line and weighted flies.

Crawdads (*year-round*). I categorize these as similar to leeches. No major gathering or school to work, but they tend to live everywhere and can be active at any time of day. You may not see them often, but many lakes have a population. I think every lake on my own list contains them, and it seems more recently that a number of good patterns are being invented. Crawdads locate around rocky shorelines and offer good fare for larger trout. I fish many of these areas in pursuit of browns, but I never use an actual crawdad pattern. No reason other than I'm a leech and minnow guy in that type of cover, and those patterns work for me. Others may prefer buggers or something similar, and those are also good choices. I certainly wouldn't discourage crawdad patterns, as I believe they work as well as anything.

Other Foods. Our list could certainly keep going, given the variety of stillwater trout food out there. Scuds (small shrimplike crustaceans) and water boatmen (bottom-swimming insects with oar-like hind legs) are just two examples of other trout foods where I live and fish. On occasion you'll find something a little less ordinary living in a lake or pond. An example I recently ran across was a very healthy population of salamanders. The mature ones were maybe 3 inches long, and they were located throughout a small mountain pond I was exploring for the first time. I spent the first two hours or so hitting 12-inch rainbows, but couldn't help thinking these salamanders would nicely feed a much larger generation of trout. On that hunch, I stuck around and worked the place over hard, looking specifically where you'd find better-sized fish. Sure enough, they were in there. Normally that many smaller fish would have convinced me there was nothing else going on, but the food source was too obvious. There had to be something much bigger making a meal out of all those salamanders.

When you find a large supply of food, you'll almost always find a large predator. Nature just works that way. So if you observe anything that would satisfy the appetite of larger fish, start looking for them with confidence. And in general, when working unfamiliar territory, look for all the visible food sources, and make an assessment of what they will most likely support (large or small, many or few).

Too good to ignore: A fertile mountain pond with a robust population of salamanders should smell of prime potential. On this day I wasn't finding much at first, but staying put into the afternoon revealed a different side of the lake's trout population, when a number of well-fed rainbows came out to play.

Do yourself a big favor, and don't let conventional fly-fishing thought rule all your decisions. It has its place, but a lot of it can often hold you back. Prime example: Insect X is visibly hatching, so I'll match it with my fly and try till I hook one; meanwhile, any further thought and innovative ideas are checked at the door. You're killing your own chances for success. A straight match may be the answer at times, while at other times it's the fastest way to get skunked. Other examples:

- Continually changing out your fly till something hits, as if the fly were the determining factor.
- Thinking a masterful cast has everything to do with it. It doesn't.
- Thinking the fish care about all that gear you upgraded to last year. They don't.
- Making WHEN–WHERE decisions based on only one or two factors instead of looking at the big picture. For example, fishing only in the morning in summer sounds reasonable—until you get skunked, give up by noon, and after you've left the damsel hatch of the century goes off between 1 and 4 p.m.

FISH BEHAVIOR AND ACTIVITY
Once you can identify WHEN and WHERE trout will be comfortable enough to hold and feed, next you'll want to interpret their behavior and activity, either by visual signs or drawing strikes, preferably both.

To start, it's good to have a big-picture understanding of how trout feed and how they select among available food sources. At any given time, a lake or pond will offer any number of foods at once. However, a single source is usually predominant. As time passes, the major food sources phase in and out—gradually, in most cases. Trout will display a lot of instinctive behavior as this happens, much of it predictable. For one, they really enjoy dinner among friends. Always look for feeding *en masse* when a significant food source occurs. For another, they tend to know ahead of time when dinner will be served. That means trout are experts at identifying upcoming trends. So as a food source cycles through, fish will abandon it early to go seek out the next major source, even at a very early stage. It's a simple reaction to anticipating what's ahead, while knowing the present source will be on its way out before long. For you and me, that means understanding why a perfectly viable food may sit idle at times, or provide much-less-than-expected action at the end of your line—assuming your execution is right. So your next move is going to be finding the new food source and figuring out the feeding schedule. You can usually find this on the same day of your current outing, but it's a matter of when. Essentially, it's a function of your schedule. If you're out all day, you stand good odds of solving this puzzle; on a partial day, you'll need a bit of luck in terms of your schedule crossing paths with the other emerging food sources.

Reading the Signs

In the event you have the advantage of visual signs, you can interpret feeding behavior by the type of movement. You'll find different versions here but I like simplicity, so I categorize them in three ways: rise, boil (or sip), and roll.

The rise is that classic "jump" that instantly raises your blood pressure and creates that new sense of urgency. It usually means they're doing a full take on top of the surface, and likely you should go with traditional dry patterns.

A boil is simply where the fish stays under the surface and just sips its food, while only slightly breaking the film. So the appearance has the effect of boiling water. A less-experienced eye will often pass this off as a smaller fish, yet much of the time boils are caused by larger fish breaking only the amount of surface necessary to feed. Less effort and more stealth are signs of older and smarter fish. If you see this where browns are present, it's time to pay a lot of attention. Think small emergers when boiling persists.

A roll may or may not break the surface, but it will at least cause a ripple visible to the eye. Sometimes it's a sign of feeding, sometimes not. I usually strip shallow, even with a sinking line, and it works.

Strikes can also give off useful behavioral information. Again I keep it simple and distinguish between two types: committed and short. Overall, you usually get one or the other at a given time—but not both—because, as noted before, fish tend to display collective behavior. The good news is that committed strikes happen the majority of the time. And committed means just that. These fish are serious about feeding, and the takes are deliberate. The majority of your hook sets will be solid, with good placement. These strikes take place the majority of the time, and if you set the hook and play the fish right, you should expect to land about 80 percent of them.

Not so with short-strikes. In fact, you may only land 20 percent of those. The short-strike can be a rather frustrating exercise, especially when a fisherman is unfamiliar with the occurrence. One fish after another, you'll miss most of the strikes and lose most of the hookups, regardless of fly selection or other method change. The ones you end up landing are generally "hooked funny"—many in places other than the mouth. The cause is likely from swatting or brushing the offering as an instinctive or territorial reaction to the sight of it.

What I'm saying is, it has nothing to do with your execution, though it may seem like it does. The fact is that the fish are just not at the active period of feeding time. My theory is they are either about to begin—or have just finished—a major meal, so they are still gathered and showing hints of those behaviors. Out of instinct, they'll phase in and out of feeding activity gradually—and you may have done a good job locating them at this in-between time. In my experience, you're best to stick with it and simply adjust your expectations for a time. Enjoy being among fish and drawing lots of reaction to your fly. About half of the time, if you hang around instead of giving up, their behavior will evolve into committed strikes. Again, this supports the theory of phasing, so if you find them ahead of dinner instead of afterward, you'll hit the jackpot. Often enough, it's worth the reward to keep your head and stay at it.

Also worth mentioning, when this has happened in the presence of other anglers, the entire group observed the same behavior among the fish (further proof that it wasn't just me!). Tips: If you suspect a short-strike situation, test it first by changing out your fly to rule out a bum hook point. Also, try leaving your fly as stunned after a miss, instead of pulling it to cast again. At times they'll "drive by," turn, and take it on the second pass.

Location

Whether or not you find a good food source to lead you to the fish, you'll need to consider where the fish themselves are actually located. When no visible signs are present, the best use of your time is to methodically section off the water in order to cover it efficiently. This starts to really matter at places like East Lake, in Central Oregon, where the surface area exceeds 1,000 acres. That's a lot of potentially empty water to search through.

In general, what works best for me is to break it down five ways: shoreline, shoal-shallow, shoal-deep, open water shallow, and open water deep. By *shoal*, I mean where the lake floor extends for a distance out from shore at a depth of no more than 10 feet or so. This depth allows good sunlight all the way to the bottom, supporting more vegetation and food. *Shallow* means depths of 5 or 6 feet, while *deep* means from that level down to 10 or 12 feet. Beyond 12 feet or so, a lot less activity goes on. However I *will* go there as a last resort if the other five sections fail to produce. (Admittedly, I seldom go there.)

The five sections can be put in any order of priority, depending on conditions. I assess everything on the spot and put these locations in order—from most likely to least likely. Really, it's not tragic to put them in the wrong order, since you can move through each location rather quickly. I estimate it only takes 5 or 10 minutes to sample a section, and you should know pretty fast whether it's active or not. Zero strikes means move on, one means try it a little longer, two means stick around a while, and so on. Search however you like; for me, the same setup works fine for all five sections. Usually I'm throwing a leech with a Type V full-sink line. *Shoreline* or *shallow* means don't count it down far, and *deep* means enjoy the scenery for a few seconds before ripping it back.

Obviously your search will be more concentrated with food around; but in the absence of good clues, I find an aggressive and efficient run through the five sections are the best use of time and the fastest way to that first strike. Put another way, the last thing you want to do is waste a lot of valuable time searching empty water. Note: I generally consider cover as part of the shoreline; therefore, much of the time when I'm "working the shoreline," I may be fishing around different types of structure just out from the bank.

While searching, you'll still want to keep watch for any possible clues in the surrounding areas. Many signs can offer clues—the presences of swallows, surface changes, lighting changes, wind direction, debris, or someone else with bent rod (one of the best clues out there; make use of it). Speaking of other anglers, I wouldn't go crowd them just because they're getting action, but do observe where and how they drew the strike: which of the five sections they were in, how deep they were, how slow or fast their retrieve, and so forth. Hint: They won't be surrounded by all the fish in the lake, so you can create the same situation for yourself without fishing next to them. With a little practice, replicating conditions is not that hard to master, and it beats being lazy. Moreover, it's good etiquette.

Search diligently enough and eventually you'll run across a good clue or a strike. And really a strike is just another form of a clue. The lesson here is to treat every strike—regardless of how random—as a source of good, viable information. Every time I fish, the first strike begets the next, which

Heavy shoreline cover like this is highly likely to hold trout. Interestingly, this particular section along a rock face will continue to produce fallen trees, given the unstable ground on top. That means even more structure for hungry trout to lurk in as time goes on.

in turn begets the one after that. I simply hop from one strike to the next, using each one as more information on WHERE to zero-in on more fish. I don't always discover what they were feeding on, or why they were gathered where I found them. It's great to figure that out, but if I don't, I can still capitalize once I know where they are. A good fly fisher can keep burying the hook without seeing the whole picture; often you only need half the picture to take full advantage.

Small Pond Characteristics and Considerations
Ponds tend to be very temperamental, appearing at times to be barren, while at other times appearing to brim over with a gross abundance of trout. Cramped living space is the reason, creating its own set of unique challenges and methods of survival. As a result, trout behavior in ponds can be quite different from that in the average lowland lake, for instance.

Sometimes food can be plentiful and easily consumed; on the other hand, good cover is often scarce, causing the majority of inhabitants to lay low under certain conditions. For you, this means not assuming a place is void of trout. But, even if your first trip to a pond might be described as hitting the jackpot, you should understand that the pond is not going to be a 24/7 gold mine. Soon enough you'll see its darker side.

When searching, look for a single, obvious clue that would suggest where fish are congregated. In a shallow pond with high visibility, the primary concern among trout may be one of security. Food may be available all day, so these fish might remain inactive for most of it, coming out to feed once or twice when conditions allow. This could be when the wind breaks up the surface; when shade is present; or early and late, when there is less daylight. If the pond seems empty, look for any shade, structure along the bank, or the deep end—if you can find it. In very small ponds, if fish are inactive, you're best off to stop and wait them out; they like to turn on and off like a light in close quarters. Ponds can also be quite unforgiving in less than prime conditions, so if an early spring trip has you kicking yourself for even bothering, come back when it warms up a little.

With any pond, you'll up your odds considerably by spending enough time on it, both in a single outing and later on. As with anywhere else, spending the better part of the day at a pond will allow more observation and enable you to cross paths with trout when they become active. In the same way, if your first sampling yields nothing but smallish trout, don't automatically assume that's all the pond has to offer. Showing a population of juvenile fish is yet another method ponds have of hiding their valuable secrets. In some cases, a pond *will* only support those undersized ones; however, half of the time, an angler just takes the sample at face value, not realizing what actually lurks there. Look for the factors that usually determine the presence of larger trout (see pages 8–10).

Likewise, consider the signs that a pond may not support anything bigger than a 9- or 10-inch fish: Overpopulation, the presence of non-trout species, weak food supply, insufficient cover, and lack of any real depth all contribute to smaller inhabitants. Ponds that dry up on occasion are usually not a good sign, either. And remember that brook trout are a prime candidate for overpopulation. They can still get big in ponds, but the likelihood is simply less than with other trout.

In any case, you can't know for sure whether a pond holds larger fish or not, so your best bet is giving it enough of a chance. Again, don't throw

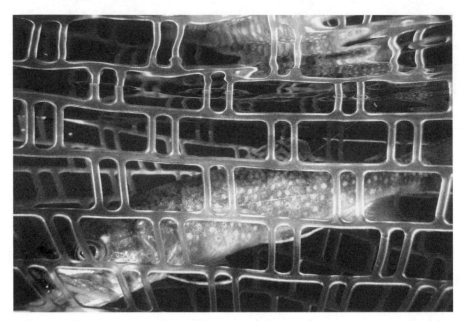

It may overpopulate and can be gullible most of the time, but no one ever accused the brook trout of being ugly.

in the towel based on a single outing or a single period of the day. You won't force these older trout to show themselves when they aren't otherwise active, so the most effective way to find them is by making it a function of time. In my experience, smaller fish may feed most of the day, while the older set will come out for a shorter duration, perhaps just at dusk or while a major food source occurs (the same behavior can occur in larger lakes). You'll recall that larger fish demand a safer feeding environment as well as more sustenance in their food selection. Therefore, their movements and timing can be far different from those of the younger members of the population. So give a pond the same consideration you would give a larger lake if you want to enjoy its rewards.

Trends

Once you have been out and have information about the water, the best use of it is to understand trends—namely that they are ever present and extremely useful. This goes back to the discussion on gradual phasing. Example: That prolific minnow infestation you observe today will be there tomorrow, probably next week, and possibly even in several weeks. However, it won't remain indefinitely and is in a constant state of change; it's

Pond patterns: You have the same flexibility with fly selection in a pond as you would most anywhere. Six Pack, Gold-Ribbed Hare's Ear, and Elk Hair Caddis are three of my own standards.

either phasing in, at its peak, or phasing out at any given time. Alongside that, the activity that surrounds those minnows will fluctuate each day or week, depending on weather changes and other factors.

Already you can see how a number of factors work together to influence the bite, and as long as you have a starting point (e.g., they were active three nights ago near dusk in X location), you can begin establishing a trend—predicting WHEN and WHERE your odds will be best. And that nicely supports the idea of getting out as often as you can, because the more times you go, the more you catch with each outing.

Trends make great predictors, but, within any trend, no two days will be exactly alike. There are simply too many factors in a constant state of movement. Any time I have fished two days in a row at the same lake, I may have had similar results at day's end, but each day would have fished differently when broken down hour by hour. Any number of small factors will continually shift around; events and occurrences don't repeat exactly day after day. Some of that sounds pretty obvious, but the point is not to assume everything will occur in the same way on a subsequent outing. Too much reliance on predictability will cause lazy thinking on Day Two, and when the six fish you hit between noon and 1 p.m. yesterday don't show up, you need to resort back to diligent observation—along with that efficient searching we were just talking about. When you can do both at once (observe trends and search diligently), you'll start consistently multiplying your results.

On a larger scale, no two years will ever repeat the same set of trends either. Think about food sources and fish activity from year to year as you would the weather. It's always different, and in fact, weather patterns are probably the most significant driver of changing trends in food and fish each year. For instance, will damsels likely show up this summer like they did last summer? Yes. But, will they go nuts at the far end of the lake at midafternoon for three hours during the last two weeks of August like last summer? Highly unlikely. They may be around during that time, but where, when, and how many will most certainly be different—along with how good the fishing is. Again, figure that those damsels should be around, but factor that in with everything else as you search; don't just show up at the far end of the lake at 2 p.m. on August 20 expecting to wear a hole into your net.

Another big factor is that disparity between your schedule and that of the fish. Unfortunately there couldn't be a bigger mismatch. You and I can only control so much of that, especially with families—and retirement nowhere in sight for most of us. But to the extent possible, living by the fish's schedule will pay big rewards. At the very least, I always try to find where my schedule will coincide with theirs. That alone has probably brought more fish to my net than anything else.

Keeping a log is a good idea to a point, as it helps establish trends and gives a feel for what generally repeats and what does not. You'll also be able to track how different combinations of weather and conditions correlate to different trout behaviors. The thing to remember here is that keeping a log has limitations. Eventually you'll want to rely less on the log and focus more on improvisation and puzzle-solving skills. Much of your success in a day will come from observing, interpreting, and using real-time occurrences as they unfold, and most of the payoff goes to those who are good at seat-of-the-pants flying.

MY BROWN TROUT OBSESSION: A CASE STUDY

Because of its unique behavior—and the rewards that go with successful pursuit—I'm going to pay the brown some extra attention here. Where I live, I seriously doubt any lack of interest exists among fly fishers when it comes to chasing and capturing the so-called golden predator. Most stories involving the great ones usually end the same way (like any good fish story). Ever notice that? Of course it only fuels the mystique of this great fish—which I happen to like.

When I first started crossing paths with browns, I assumed their appearance was incidental—and not very frequent—while you were fishing for other species of trout. To me, that meant the best way to catch a brown was by pure luck while chasing other trout; they'd just come around when they felt like it. I was wrong.

Eventually I began to notice the unique traits of browns and their behavior, at about the same time I was taking a big interest in trout behavior in general. I was just getting on to the idea that studying behavioral habit was a worthwhile discipline, with rewards I couldn't ignore. What followed was an infatuation with the wary predator that brought on countless hours of fishing in the dark, the light, the depths, the cover—you name it. I looked for them anywhere they might live, hold, or feed.

For the first time in years, I began using a log to track my progress. Every brown landed or missed was recorded on a spreadsheet, along with any factual data I could identify about the occurrence—time, date, temperature, location, size, fly, etc. On another spreadsheet, I began mining all the stocking data in my state, creating a ten-year historical graph of every lake that held browns. Then, on subsequent tabs, I recorded all the written information I could find on browns in local waters.

In a couple of years, the file paid off big. All the data gathered in the first year was used to give chase in the second, and my results more than doubled. In the third year, the same thing happened, and the trend continued. Overall, what they say about this fish is true in terms of its superiority among trout, along with the greater challenge—as compared with the other species—in finding and fooling the brown. But interestingly, once the behavioral differences are understood, a brown can be pursued methodically and somewhat predictably, with consistent results.

Tales of Giants and Monsters. You know what I mean here: those stories of prehistoric behemoths that only awaken in the dark of night to take oversized streamers. This hunt is not exactly for the faint at heart. Any fisher with less than a 10-inch streamer should probably just stay home. Well, I'd love to tell you these fish are all over the place out there, and that you need only go out after dark with the biggest minnow pattern available for the legend to become a reality. Problem is, no one's camera seems to work after dark—or something like that. There just isn't a lot of proof floating around that these giants are being caught. And you and I both know mortal man just isn't strong enough to hold his tongue with such a great secret.

Here's what I know: Yes, those fish exist in our lakes. However, their behavior and movements are best described as random, and they are generally caught when some lucky fisherman crosses their path at the right time and place (usually by day). At that size, their needs are significantly different from those of smaller fish, so these giants are forced to live quite differently. Can their particular habits be learned and understood in such a way as to make them predictable on some level? My best answer is, anything is possible; but the smaller numbers of these fish, along with the ways they move about and feed, make the game and your odds much different than when pursuing average-size browns or other species of trout. By "much different," I mean much less in your favor. For me, learning and understanding your average brown, which still grows quite large, will probably give you the best odds of crossing paths with a legend.

Stillwater browns have been known to grow faster than their moving-water cousins owing to the difference in conditions and food availability in lakes. Also, their ability to adapt better to an environment and feed more efficiently than rainbows, for example, really does make them superior. Not

Expect the unexpected: True, I was looking for browns this time, but you never know what you're going to get. This oversized largemouth was more than a surprise in a lake reported to hold only trout.

surprisingly, the evolution of the brown suggests just this. It's simply an older fish species with a past that involves more adaptation than other trout.

Generally speaking, the time I have spent pursuing browns has mostly reinforced what I've read about them. The good news is that they are certainly catchable and can be had with regularity. And though their behavior may differ from that of other trout, it can be just as easily learned—as can their movements and timing. Here we'll apply some of the material covered so far and see how it pertains to browns.

Behavior. This is everything. It's what makes the brown such a worthwhile target, and it's why the fish is so interesting. If you're waiting for that brush with the prehistoric monster we all hear about, you and your oversized white streamer will probably wait around a long time. And you'll miss what makes this fish so great to pursue. The real fun is in learning how different browns can be from other trout and then using that knowledge to go after them. The best place to start is territory, as the brown stands out among others when it comes to possessing and protecting its home space. We see this in its attack methods and its tendency to occupy cover alone, refusing to be moved from it. The brown remains wary and is easily spooked; however, once you've presented well to one, you often can't get away from it—even if you wanted to. A brown will display aggressive behavior to the point that all its caution is thrown to the wind, but the angler may have to get him there through such means as body placement, stealth, going in soft and coming out hard with your fly, playing to his field of vision, looking for opportunities in low visibility, and so on.

More on Timing. While it's a subset of behavior, I'd say timing is the most notable part of a brown's behavior. Again, the general rules certainly apply, so start there: Middle temperatures in the spring and fall really are best, but browns will show year-round. Low lighting and generally limited visibility are important factors, and evening is king. Summer months tend to be the slowest time of year, given the higher water temperatures. Where migration and spawning take place, browns will move into the streambeds to spawn in fall, typically in October. The larger ones are commonly sought

Browns are not exactly easy, but always worth it. Note that they come calling and are landed or lost before your brain is able to process it. That means catching them is exciting, so it's a good idea to plan mentally for both scenarios and, to the extent possible, expect both outcomes as regular parts of the game. For me, win or lose, the game is always a privilege to play, and I'm always grateful just to have a shot at one.

after by fly fishers at this time of year. Once spawning takes place, usually in November, the fish will begin feeding aggressively and will remain in the rivers throughout winter until re-entering the lakes in spring.

Methodology. Though their behavior and habits can be unique, where and how you fish for browns are often very similar to location and technique for fishing other trout. The differences are more about timing and available opportunity—those being much more limited in the case of browns. In terms of location, they certainly don't stick to one type of area, so I wouldn't assume you have to look deep and in cover to find them. Like any other fish, their movements are driven by food availability, temperature, and considerations for stealth and safety. That said, I've hit them literally everywhere—shallow, deep, along shore, in the open, tight to cover, you name it. Think of it this way, they shop at the same stores and eat at the same restaurants as other trout, just at different times, and they usually don't hang out as long. Keep that in mind and you'll do well chasing them.

Although you'll find some overlap with other species of trout when it comes to how to search for browns, the different aspects of location are still worth a look here. Understanding the various similarities and differences between browns and other trout can be a helpful tool when learning to target browns specifically.

Shoreline. Perhaps the favorite and best-known location among those who hunt browns, the bank can sometimes be one of the most fun and productive areas to find them. Spring, fall, and evenings are best prospecting times, but really there's only one way to find out if they're in at any given moment—go give it a shot. Often they can be spotted along shore by surface activity; at other times they may be in thick, but no visible signs exist. If you go in with confidence, you can determine their presence fairly easily. About 15 or 20 minutes should be plenty of time, and if you find one during that period, you can find more. Otherwise, if there are no signs or strikes in that amount of time, you're usually best off to search elsewhere. Just remember, browns can turn on and off like a light along shore at any given time, so you're best to go in regularly and not let the bank sit idle for too long.

Open Water. The most productive, yet often the most overlooked location for browns. What I mean by open water is, if you're not against the shoreline, you're in open water. Given its size and complexity compared to shore, the open water can be somewhat of a mystery and a bit overwhelming when conducting a search. I suspect the reason a lot of searching takes place along shore is due to its easy access and familiarity, not so much because it's the place to be at a given time. Along with that, much of the talk would lead you to believe that's where you find browns. However, if you do get all yours along shore, you're easily missing most of what's available, big and small.

Surface Feeding. This can happen anywhere, along shore or out in the open. Browns may feed on just about anything that breaks through the film or sits on top of the lake surface. Among the best food sources to watch for are hatching *Callibaetis*, given their large size and prolific numbers, particularly in spring. A good *Callibaetis* population can sustain and provide a primary food source for browns for up to several weeks. Regardless of the food source, when browns are visibly present at the surface, a good fly fisher will observe and take note of the type of motion, or form of rise, they display. Remember that surface feeding can show in the form of a rise, boil, or roll.

The Depths. This means down a few feet, not way down where it's deep and dark. Browns don't need to lurk where it's cold and tough to breathe. Like other fish, they don't have good reason to hang out there either. Food, oxygen, and other comforts appeal to them just the same. So

Pablo's Cripple is a menace to any brown seeking surface fare, even the smart ones. And no need to be bashful in the presence of giants, as this small emerger works for brown trout of any size.

when searching at depth, I like to sweep the outer shoals and places just beyond. Near a drop-off is also a good bet. And if searching in much deeper water, I'll still work in that 10- to 15-foot range instead of way down. Fishing these areas tends to be a slower, more methodical grind compared with shallow places. That's OK if it produces action.

Other Locations. Not all lakes and reservoirs are created equal in terms of available habitat. Wherever you hunt for browns, be sure and familiarize yourself right away with the various terrains and structures your chosen lake has to offer. Where stream inlets exist, you'll want to spend regular time in their immediate area. Newly oxygenated water, cooler temperatures, and food supplies are associated with inlets. That's no guarantee fish will be present, but many times they'll congregate there for the preceding reasons. Where the information is available (usually by bathymetric map or your depth finder), I'd put some work in along any drop-offs; here's where browns often find temperature change along with diversification of food sources. I tend to search drop-offs with a full sinking line using a cast-count-strip approach (more on methods later).

One other location to pay special attention to is any man-made structure. On one of my local lakes, I regularly search out browns near docks, parked boats, and even the retaining walls that front some of the residential property. A structure may not strike you as a worthwhile or natural habitat, but man-made cover works exactly the same as anything else where browns are concerned. Another thing we care about that they don't.

Night Hours. No guarantee they'll be active simply because it's dark outside; however, browns, particularly large ones, tend to be synonymous with the disappearance of daylight. First tip: When night fishing, I'd include either dusk or first light as a priority, depending on when you fish. Often these transitions between night and day will spur activity, even when all other hours were less than ideal on the bite. Next tip: Although browns can be found in a variety of places at night (all of the above locations can apply), you may have a little more fun prioritizing the shoreline or any good structure when you search. If found lurking there, browns are often holding in wait to ambush anything that happens by; that combination of darkness and cover is ideal for larger fish in search of larger food. In my experience, some of the most aggressive attacks by some of the largest browns occur there. This is also when those big streamers come in handy. Minnow patterns are commonplace, and many times I prefer some of our local saltwater and sea-run cutthroat patterns over typical lake flies. Deceiver and Imitator baitfish patterns are among my favorites. Fish them right against shore, and don't be afraid to make a splash or retrieve unusually fast. You stand a better chance of drawing their interest than of spooking them in this circumstance, and you can't outrun them by stripping too rapidly.

This lesson has been about locating trout in a stillwater environment. If you did it right, you've come in with a good plan based on timing, conditions, and maybe the current trends, and that's solved half of the puzzle. Good so far. Next you've observed, interpreted, and made good use of everything going on around you at the lake—and now all the pieces are finally there. All that's left is putting them in place, and the day's puzzle is finished. Of all the elements of stillwater fly fishing you can master, understanding the details of WHEN and WHERE will affect how often you bury the hook more than any other skill.

Lesson 3

TACTICS AND TECHNIQUES

Locating fish may come as a higher priority as far as your success is concerned, but execution is probably more fun to read (and write) about. So now we shift to the HOW–WHAT part of our equation. In basic terms, we're talking about HOW to execute and WHAT to use, which refer mostly to fly selection but also include lines, leaders, and such. Being able to consistently increase your catch does not come from some revolutionary new method of luring fish; rather success comes when a number of seemingly subtle differences are brought together and put into practice. The tough part is, you can't tell by looking at an angler that he's doing anything different from the next guy—except that he spends more time with rod bent. Those subtleties are simply the methods by which he searches for fish and then goes about presenting to them.

EXECUTION AND STRATEGY

Execution can mean a lot of things on the water. Here I'll discuss some of the tangible ones that I have found most useful. Some parts of searching can overlap with execution, so perhaps that's the best place to start.

If you'll recall, we talked about every strike being a useful piece of information for solving the puzzle. Again, whether you draw one by accident or by following clues, you can now start making conclusions about where fish may be grouped *en masse*. In that way, I always try to turn a strike into several—or even more. This means considering everything you can about the hit: depth, retrieve, nearby structure, existence of food, time of day, lighting, surface chop—the list goes on. If you think about it, a single strike provides a multitude of clues, yet all too often, these aren't considered. And much in the same way, drawing no strike is also a valuable clue, since knowing what is not working can be every bit as helpful.

We also touched on the fact that results are determined by available opportunities. With this in mind, it's best to show up with some flexibility about your expectations for the day. An easy mistake is expecting X number of fish because you got that yesterday, or because it is late spring and conditions are prime. Problem is, trout are simply never that predictable. If anything, they are masters of keeping you and me guessing. Part of good puzzle-solving is recognizing limitations and accepting them for what they are.

Fishing Smarter

I'd love to tell you the perfect presentation is achievable, or that it's possible to be perfect as a fly fisher, but neither will happen on this planet. So if you can't be perfect, the next best thing is being smart. That means giving yourself the best odds, and maximizing your results—given the circumstances and your capabilities. For example, you spot a handful of fish visibly feeding in one area and commit to raising one. Numerous attempts go by, along with several fly changes, and nothing works. No strikes, no interest, nothing. What's worse, you can't figure out the formula, or why they won't take interest.

OK, stop right there. First, are there other opportunities nearby that might hold better odds for you? Chances are, if you see these fish feeding, they aren't the only ones doing so. Maybe they're the only ones you can see, but that's not saying much. Who knows what's under the surface all around you. So is it the best use of your time to win (or die trying) against the ones you're casting to, or are you better off accepting defeat and moving on? Well, since you and your presentation have proven to be less than perfect (again that's OK), you can still redeem yourself by being smart.

Think of it this way: Two anglers are put into that same situation. One stays, and the other accepts defeat and moves on. An hour later, the die-hard has nothing to show for it, while his partner has picked up four by working the open water at a few feet of depth. Who would you rather be? Does it matter that the second guy was a quitter and never figured out the solution to those risers? Or was he smart enough to make the best of the hand he was dealt? Who ended up catching fish?

Time Management

Now that you're on the water with open-minded expectations, one of the most effective tactics you can use in a day is time management. Unfortunately this effective weapon gets overlooked or entirely forgotten by most. I'm sure the majority of anglers would rather lose track of the time when on the water. Can't say I blame anyone for that, but I also can't ignore how useful the watch is as a tool for catching fish. As a trend-monitoring tool, I use one constantly to track progress throughout the day, to observe when and how long any feeding goes on, and to track the timing of the appearance of any food sources.

And I use my watch even more to search efficiently. If I'm not drawing strikes, I closely limit the time I allow for each searching method or area covered. If, for example, I decide to work the shoreline, I'll probably give it 15 minutes—20 tops—without a strike before abandoning the idea. Usually that's all the time you'll need to determine whether you're on fish or not. That way, you can sample a good variety of water within a reasonable time, usually less than an hour. A skilled fly fisher can usually find action, or determine that it's slow, within 30 minutes to an hour. Point being, don't spend whole hours doing the same thing if it's not producing. You're always better off trying three or four things in that amount of time. Note: You may find some of the numbers I use aren't necessarily the best ones for you. So, if 20 minutes doesn't allow a thorough search for you, by all means use 30, or 40, or whatever works best. We don't all cover water at the same pace, or with the same level of confidence.

Other Anglers

We already discussed how much information you can gain by observing everything you can when another guy hits one. To take that a step further, pay attention to everyone around you all day. There are lots of clues to be had just by watching who is doing what, and I'd pay attention to more than *who* is catching fish. Also watch *how* everyone fishes. Each will cover water differently and make a unique presentation.

On my first visit to a new lake, I started out with a sinking line working the mid and lower depths. Soon I observed another guy tearing the place up, while the minutes ticked by for me without so much as a bump. About 15 minutes of that was more than enough. I set the rod down, poured a cup, and watched my new friend work. It took me an entire 30 seconds to figure out he was using a floating line and emerger. And since there were no visible signs of food or shallow feeding, my only clue was the other fisher and his bent rod. Another 3 whole minutes and I was re-rigged, cast out, and first fish on.

Remember, just using the same fly as the successful fisher won't do it. Observe everything someone is doing if he's having success, particularly where and how the strikes are coming. A final tip: If you go out and a number of fishers are there, look around and size them up. Maybe you even recognize one or two of them. Decide who might offer the best clues that day. But pay attention to everyone, since those *not* getting action are also helpful. I always think of it as a group effort, and eight fishers can cover water much more effectively than one. So think of those seven others as your team from now on.

Fishing Together. No doubt, one of the best ways to enjoy our sport is with fellow fly fishers. There's no wrong way to enjoy time spent with friends, but it's easy to fish at half-throttle on those days. In fact, I spent a number of years believing that whenever I wanted to get serious, I had to fish alone. Well, I wasn't exactly right to think that, or to think that I was the only one interested in ripping it up every time out. The more people I fish with, the more I realize most of us want both the camaraderie and lots of fish. My suggestion is, exchange whatever notes, observations, and ideas you have before putting in and then split up. As enjoyable as the side-by-side experience can be, it's anything but effective. Each of you fishing your own way, while having full concentration, makes for a strong team if you pay attention to one another. I've even been known to make cellphone calls back and forth when a friend is out of sight and something is worth sharing.

Notes on Experience Levels. Two or more of you, reasonably matched, can usually split up and make quick work of the place. However, I always recommend a game-change if experience levels are further apart. If you happen to be the more skilled, drop the career day and lend your partner a hand. You have a much better opportunity in front of you—as I consider fly fishing's highest honor and best accomplishment to be the assistance of another in his or her success. A good fly fisher buries the hook with his own hands, but a great one can bury the hook with someone else's hands. Point is, helping another fisher out is anything *but* a wasted outing; anytime I see a friend hit one on my advice, the reward is ten-fold over doing it myself.

If you happen to be the one less skilled, learn all you can from your friend without cramping his style. Respect that he may want to enjoy tearing it up, in addition to helping you out. Ask a few questions, and then spend the rest of the time observing. If your more skilled friend wants to spend more time working with you, by all means take advantage and be grateful. In short, set your rod down and help those who are less skilled, but don't expect it when the tables are turned. You always want other anglers to be glad they went with you.

About the Fly
Overrated. To start, we're talking about trout. The more you take an interest in this creature and pursue an understanding, the more you'll realize how complex trout behavior really is. It's not about what trout eat. They eat anything they can catch, size notwithstanding. Food doesn't need to look good, taste good, or be the right color—it just needs to fit down its throat.

Recall everything we've discussed so far. We've already considered a multitude of factors, including practically living your life in a certain way to get that fly in front of a hungry fish—hopefully a good crowd of them. So if you've made it that far, you can throw practically anything at a trout and draw the take. Present it with confidence and give it life, and that fish is yours. (Of course, your ability to locate and present to them may be a different story.) There are always exceptions, but, most of the time, trout aren't that finicky about food in stillwater.

I tend to select flies based on general size and appearance, along with how they cast and move in the water. And when food is present, I may or may not match the size and appearance of it. Either way—matching or not matching—can prove effective, depending on a lot of factors; but by far the most important thing about the fly you select is *you*. Ever go to a pattern and immediately feel it was the wrong choice? Ever notice how you present a fly when you're not 100 percent confident in it? The minute you lose confidence in a fly, get rid of it. I wouldn't waste a single cast on a presentation I don't believe in. Often without you realizing it, your lack of confidence will greatly affect your presentation, and though your odds may not go to zero, they'll still plummet.

Fundamentally, I don't find choosing a food acceptable to a fish to be where the sport is—not in the case of trout. To me, understanding trout well enough to locate, lure, and capture them time after time, in an endless chaos of circumstances, is exactly where the sport is. The fly, along with rod, reel, and line, is just a fun way of burying the hook after the real game has been played out. My point is, think what you will of the fly, but look well beyond it—or you'll never know how much you're missing.

PRESENTATIONS

With presentation methods I tend to go the simple route: Less is more.

Fly Line

There is no hard and fast rule on what you should use or how many different lines you should carry. The more I fish stillwater, the less variety I depend on. At present, I use the same Type V sinker 95 percent of the time year round. Anymore, with the density-compensated lines in use today, you get a lot of versatility out of a single line. And in my case, I lean hard toward more aggressive presentations. For me, even a shallow approach can be made effectively with a fast sinker at times, simply by not counting it down.

Beyond my Type V, the remaining 5 percent of the time is when the floater comes out for drys, or when nymphs or streamers are presented very close to the surface, and either that or the slow sink is used. But for the most part, I like saving the Type II for shallow ponds and such; I feel the same way about some of the clear camo and sinking tips. I don't find them to be of much use, and in stillwater I don't see the logic in the curve of a sinking tip. In the absence of any current to negotiate, why not have a straight-line connection when you set the hook? Again, the rules are not rigid, and I'm simply sharing what works best for me in my surroundings when it comes to fly lines. The argument for a sinking tip, for example, is certainly debatable, and most importantly, if this or anything else I don't subscribe to is productive for you, by all means stay with it.

Cast-Count-Strip

Most times I prefer to search for, and present to, fish on the retrieve or strip. In doing so, I can dial in via the depth I count down to and the speed of my retrieve (shallow fast retrieve for aggressive feeding just below surface, and so on). One of the main staples in my game is the method I use to work a sinker, and in my opinion, the results are significant. For one, the rod tip is kept submerged below the surface at all times when retrieving. In this manner your tip won't bounce when stripping; also your connection to the fly is far more direct, so you'll feel everything down to the slightest brush of a

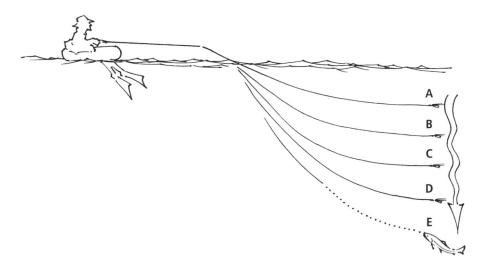

Cast-count-strip. Simple as it sounds, this method is responsible for more than 90 percent of the fish I take. Once I have determined the location and general depth of active fish, I'll go to this method to zero in. When presenting with a full-sink line, simply "count down" to the desired depth. *A* might be a couple of feet below the surface, while *E* could be a depth of 12 or 15 feet. Spend some time with your full-sink, and you'll soon develop a feel for depth as it drops. A full-sink line will allow you to search a range of depths, and if you find yourself often in the same circumstance, the different sink-rate options offer the ability to better specialize at a desired depth and speed of retrieve. And remember, you're just trying to place your fly within your target's field of vision and invite the fish to give chase. Most takes happen during the retrieve rather than on the drop.

weed. If you currently retrieve with your tip above the surface, my advice would be to submerge it and never look back. It matters that much.

For another, my stripping motion is usually fast with a long stroke—too long to gather the line on an apron, so I've adapted to letting the slack fall into the water next to me. The advantage is, the line tends to come back up without tangling when I cast out. The main disadvantage is how often the line can wrap around my leg, which I've largely solved. The problem was that the line would hang up on my fin straps instead of sliding off my foot cleanly; I had to waste time trying to free it up. To keep the line from catching, I took an old pair of socks, cut the toes open, and then slid them over my feet and ankles to cover the back half of my fins. Essentially it smoothes out the area from fins to ankles, and the line can slide freely over it. Sounds

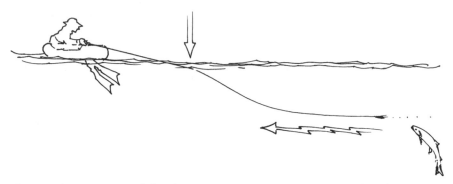

Always submerge your rod tip when presenting or retrieving a subsurface fly. You could keep it above the surface for any of several reasons; none of them are good.

odd, I know, but it's probably the best invention ever, considering the way I fish.

Another issue occurs when playing fish once hooked. With my method, all the slack is in the water instead of coiled on an apron, but I don't find it a problem for fish to move through or around it. With slack coiled on an apron, my concern would be having it tangle if the fish runs. Note that I don't play fish on the reel, so retrieving creates slack. More on that later.

Drys

I love presenting this way but, in reality, most opportunity in stillwater is underneath the surface. Generally I save drys for visible feeding at surface and rarely—if ever—search with them. Searching with drys can work and be a lot of fun, especially along the shoreline, but I haven't found them to produce as well as searching underwater. When visible feeding is present, it can take some experimentation to dial it in each time; however, dry fly fishing tends to require more of a matching strategy than subsurface presentation. I see this as a matter of cautious instinct for the fish; the closer to surface or more visible they are, the less liberal they become about what they'll strike at.

Timing is everything with drys on stillwater. Strikes can come in several ways, so your hook set will need to follow suit. In general, you'll need to develop a short hesitation when strikes occur. The trick is not to set too fast or too slow. I'll try to explain the physics here. You'll find several versions of this, but the idea is generally the same. When taking insects at surface, a trout will "vacuum in" its food and swallow it whole. The important distinction is that he does not chomp down, so the fly floats loosely as it enters the fish's mouth. That hesitation on the hook set allows its mouth to close down behind the loose fly just as the fish is about to swallow. That means, when you attempt to set your hook too quickly, you literally pull the fly back out of the trout's mouth before it can close down on it. But give it that extra fraction of a second, and you'll often pull the fly nicely back into its lip. However, wait too long and you stand good odds of the fly coming back out because of the line attached to it. Maybe the fish expels it consciously, maybe not; the result is the same.

The length of the hesitation is best developed by getting the feel through trial and error. On the hook set itself, I find softer is better. We could have a full discussion here, but the endgame is that, with drys, more will stick if you go the soft route. And regarding missed strikes, if you determine it's not your bad timing, go to another pattern that sits differently on the water. A good bet is either going smaller or using an emerger. That hook hanging beneath the surface film is deadly for catching on lips. Acknowledged, an emerger is also a very effective imitation, but I like the improved hook-up ratio it can offer in many circumstances.

Trolling

Learn to fish stillwater this way if you like. Learn your way around certain lakes this way if you like. Then get rid of it. To sum up trolling: it works and you'll catch fish, but if that's all you do, you'll never be well versed in stillwater. The sad truth is, you'll limit yourself to a small fraction of the fish that can be had, and miss everything that makes stillwater such a great pursuit. That said, trolling has its place in an outing. By saying get rid of it I mean get rid of making it your mainstay, and only troll when it makes sense.

I use trolling three ways: in tandem with retrieves to search deep, to move between casts, and simply to commute or relocate to another area. The first two are really partial trolls, since I'm only going a few yards before stripping back up. Trolling is a quick and effective way to check the entire depth range as you move between casts, and often I've hit fish and changed my approach based on unexpected strikes. The way I do it is simple: Cast, move 20 or 30 yards while your line sinks, and then strip it back up. Sounds too easy—and it is—but I can't emphasize enough how effective it can be. It's a great way to search outer shoals and open water. Pay attention to depth on any strikes. Did they hit while your line was still sinking, deep during the drag, or somewhere on the way up when stripping? Try to establish a pattern this way, and then change your approach to exploit the exact depth and presentation.

Stillwater Chironomid Fishing

For our purposes, I'm introducing this method and providing a basic understanding of how it works. Chironomid fishing is practically an entire separate pastime within fly fishing, having its own following. As you can imagine, this is yet another subject that can fill entire books by itself. The method generally involves a floating line, strike indicator (bobber), usually a long leader, and a closely matching pattern. The game is to locate the best concentrations of feeding trout at the proper depth, and present the fly either still or at a very slow motion. It gets trickier when trout are feeding primarily on the bottom, since this technique may require a very long leader. This makes the cast and playing fish more of a challenge.

As an alternative and certainly a simpler method, you can start with a floater and dry fly, and tie a length of leader to the bend in the hook to suspend a Chironomid pattern a few feet below. The dry fly serves as an indicator; it is known to get smacked on occasion, much to the surprise of the angler, though not as often as the second fly below. These rigs tend to work

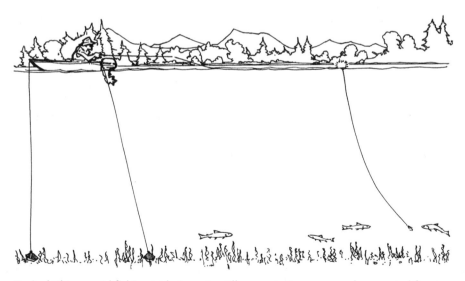

Typical Chironomid fishing technique. In still presentation, commonly executed from an anchored boat or pram, the fly is suspended via a long leader from a floating line. Since takes often cannot be seen, most Chironomid fishers prefer to use a strike indicator that floats above the leader.

Two examples of common Chironomid patterns: Red-Butt Black Buzzer (UK) and Red Ice Cream Cone.

best when running a shorter length of leader to fish fairly shallow, and they present with reasonable stealth when it matters. I can recall an outing at Halliford Mere Lakes in the United Kingdom, when a number of good-size rainbows were active in the shallows. A small black buzzer, run maybe 30 inches down from a Sedge pattern, kept me busy for some time. The method was simple to execute, and although these trout were in rather visible water, I could approach them from land and place a still presentation directly into the zone without too much disturbance.

Chironomid anglers tend to use an anchored boat or pram to accommodate the still presentation. Worth contemplating: Beyond the selection of a pattern, a Chironomid fisher's method can yield big results at times due purely to placement. Bottom feeding is the best example. If you think about it, when trout are active right along the lake floor, what better method is there for entering and staying in the strike zone? A fly suspended from a measured leader right off the bottom will hold the zone more effectively than any other approach. In comparison, a sinking line and moving presentation simply won't hold a single position the same way. However, the tables can easily turn when activity moves up in the water column and spreads out. Then the ability to move and cover more water will better serve the angler. Both methods can prove deadly at different times, often one right before the other if feeding behavior suddenly alters.

Give it life: On retrieves, you'll want to develop a feel for your presentation, even when you can't see it underwater. I liken it to seeing the fly with your hands. It's like that hesitation we were talking about on hook sets; the best way to get it is time and practice. Eventually you'll have good control over how your fly moves through the water without having to see it. Early on, your brain won't make that connection and, though you can still catch fish, you'll have a severe handicap. Making your fly lifelike really matters, and it's another great example of those undetectable things you can do to catch more fish than the next guy.

Shoreline Execution

Unlike open water, against shore you're often casting into a very small space or working a specific piece of cover. On each cast, make sure to square up to shore (like shooting a basketball) and avoid kicking backward as you cast—a common bad habit. Learn to stay still and also to keep a low profile. Many of these fish are very shallow and easily spooked when against shore, so how you move about and cast will matter a great deal. I find it best to have full control of the presentation, so I'm not afraid to get a little closer. The trick is staying aware of how I move and not doing anything to disturb the fish. It follows that less visibility (low lighting, surface chop, and so on) gives you more wiggle room, and vice versa. Just pay attention to all that stuff. In windier conditions you'll have to a get a feel

Working the cover: Christian Brewer on shoreline patrol. Here his pontoon serves as a slow moving platform for casting, while a light wind moves him along, parallel to the bank.

for compensating with casts and movement. In my experience, wind won't chase the fish out, but it may make them less bashful with the reduced visibility. So it's worth the trouble. As always, these details matter far more than the pattern you decide to throw.

More on body placement: Put simply, are you positioning yourself where you should be casting instead? Sounds insultingly obvious, but I see anglers doing it almost every time out. Consider where *you* sit any time you are casting to where you think fish are located. Is there a chance they could be right underneath you? A surprisingly common example is trolling right against shore. Much of the time you're only in 2 to 3 feet of crystal-clear water. How do you run over the top of anything that shallow and expect it to stick around and take your offering 10 seconds later? Another example of when not to troll. Instead, try staying out and casting in.

Field of Vision
One of my favorites. Think of your target's field of vision, not just its location. The idea here is to work the area the trout can see, not to thump it on the head with your cast. So when casting to shore, don't pull out just because you threw short and placed it several feet out. Try leaving it and working the retrieve as usual. In some cases that's even a better cast, as you still put it in the trout's field of vision while managing not to spook it by landing the fly too close. When in open water, consider the location of a sighted fish and think the same way. Instead of hitting it in the head, or casting past it to come back by, place your fly gently a few feet on your side of the target. Give it a short stunned pause, and then rip it back away from him. Prey that lands a few feet away from a fish then takes off in the other direction is what puts it on the offensive as a predator (and that's what you want). So avoid serving it up and, instead, make the trout work for it. A fish is used to that. Having a slab of meat fall into its lap or hit it in the face is anything but natural. Often that's why a seemingly perfect cast is not so perfect in drawing the take.

Speaking of predatory instinct: Thinking of trout as voracious predators instead of cautious survivalists is not a bad mental framework. You still have to be smart about spooking them, but there is a time to consider them as more shark-like. Forcing them to give chase by going to a bigger pattern or faster retrieve can be deadly when used at the right time. I find it works surprisingly often, as trout don't survive and grow by being timid.

Pond Skills

There can be an overwhelming amount of structure in certain lakes and ponds. Likewise, you'll run across an annoying number of snags in these places. Beyond using your old gear and fly lines, you'll do well to keep track of the more prevalent snags for the sake of both casting and playing fish. In fact, when working the shoreline, I always scan the water for submerged logs and branches that might create problems. A good skill to develop in small water is the ability to read subsurface obstacles and find the open lanes where clean retrieves can be made. Sounds like a lot of tedious work, but you'd be surprised at what lives in all that mess. Learn to fish through it and you'll be glad you did. Nevertheless, trout are experts at hanging anglers up; they will be more than happy to steal your flies and tippet, not to mention your patience and sense of humor. I'd still advise using a sinker most of the time, but a slow or intermediate sink rate is sometimes best suited for small water with its shallow depths.

A Few Tips on Snags

Flies. Bring plenty of extras. But with a little practice, you can actually free most of them up. In most cases, I reel up when moving toward a stuck fly. Sinking lines love to hang up behind you when dealing with snagged flies. Once snagged, your first try should be a simple pull in the direction the fly came from. This will free up about a third of them. If that doesn't work, see if the fly is within arm's length, roll up your sleeve, and carefully go after it. If you're too deep, try working the rod tip down to the fly and gently poking it free. This one works most of the time, but be really careful about your rod tip. Again, use the old rod for ponds. If you need to break off, use your hands, not the rod, to pull back. Even with a straight back motion, your tip is at risk. When possible, grab the leader, as it's never a good idea to pull on your fly line; only do that as a last resort. For one thing, it's easier than you think to damage or alter a fly line; for another, a leader or tippet section is much more affordable to replace.

Lines. Line slack likes to hang up almost as much as your fly. Some branches lay unattached and can simply be lifted to the surface, where your line can be easily unwrapped. If not, try going in reverse from the direction that hung it up. If the line stays hung up in any direction, clip your fly and carefully pull it all the way through. It usually comes right out, but you'll have to re-rig through your guides. At that point, I'm always grateful just to have the line back in one piece. Fortunately, I've only hung a line up completely one time. Your two options there are going for a swim, or writing a $70 check to the fly shop.

Fish. I hate this one. Your chances of getting your line free are 50/50 at best. The obvious first fix is avoidance, but the real world and the fish often have other plans. Horizontal logs give better odds, since the fish will usually just go under and can come back out the same way. I've pulled them out at times, and at other times have run the tip down next to the log for a cleaner pull through. With vertical structure, it gets a lot trickier. Once the fish goes around, it will naturally try to keep swimming away. However, your tippet will have it attached and swimming in circles like a tetherball. Round and round he'll go, wrapping around that branch until you can basically give up on the idea of working the fish loose. With good visibility and a shallow snag, you might have odds of unwrapping it, but don't count on it. If the fish hangs up at depth, popular wisdom says to wait and see if he'll come out on his own. It's worth a try, but I can't say I have a good

A network of fallen trees and submerged logs may make for challenging angling but also provides excellent trout cover. You may lose plenty of flies and spend much of your time hung up at first, but the rewards are worth gaining the skills necessary to fish around structure.

history with that one. Give it a minute or two, and then call it a stalemate. Your time is better spent getting the next one, and that fish stands a better chance of survival.

You. Not as bad as it may sound, but expect your feet and ankles to come in contact regularly. In smaller ponds, debris is commonly found just under the surface and may even brush the underside of your tube. In my experience you'll either slide right over or bounce off it, depending on how solid it is and how high up it sits. If you get concerned about what's in your path, take your net and use it as a bumper beneath the surface.

PLAYING AND RELEASING FISH

In many cases, you can leave the expensive aircraft-grade reels to those who hunt larger game. Steelheaders need them; we usually don't. In fact, using your reel to play most fish in lakes is not the best idea. I've done it plenty of times both ways, and playing away from the reel is by far more effective. The only advantage you have when using your reel is the absence of loose line behind you, but it ends there. Away from the reel, you have many times more control over retrieval speed, line tension, and slack—and they all matter a lot. When your fish runs toward you, it's nearly impossible to keep up via the reel crank. Fly reels are inherently slow, large arbors included. When the fish runs out, your skilled hands can regulate the proper amount of tension on a real-time basis. No fly reel in existence can accomplish that, but your fingers can do it quite nicely.

And regarding slack, I have never seen anglers who play on the reel do it without compromising line tension at least once. Problem is, one time is way too many. Once hooked, your fish should never get the advantage of any slack. That's an automatic get-out-of-jail-free card for him; every fish you land that was given slack was taken by pure luck.

Note that I'm saying "in most cases" when referring to non-use of the reel. In some areas, there are lakes and reservoirs where the trout are exceptional in both size and strength (or energy). Here you might be wise to rethink the above argument for playing them away from the reel. In the Pacific Northwest, we tend to see these fish in our rivers, not so much in stillwater; however, in other regions, trout of similar size and characteristics can most certainly be found in a lake setting.

A final word about reel versus no reel: if you consistently land 80 per-cent or more of your hookups while using the reel, you can ignore everything I just said. If not, do yourself a favor and rethink it. Beyond the 20 percent you should expect to lose, you're giving everything else away for no reason. Think of everything you've done to earn that hook set. Why would you give it away so easily?

You can also swing the odds your way by playing the fish closer to you. On every hook set, I either bring the fish toward me or I'll move toward it if it's stubborn. Ultimately, I want that fish very close or even underneath me. He's already spooked, so I'm not so worried about that. The farther away he is, the more wiggle room he has to maneuver. In close, they tend to jump less, as well. When I can, I'll get them 8 to 10 feet from my rod tip and then work them as much as I can with the rod, rather than letting them take slack. And along those lines, I prefer to keep the rod tip more parallel to the surface instead of raised high. This gives me more control, particularly on larger or stronger fish. Also, the larger and more aggressive the fish, the more you'll have to wait till it's ready. You'll know when; just don't force it up. Most of mine break surface without thrashing about, but I won't wait long enough to wear them out, either. There's a good balance, and after enough fish, you'll figure it out pretty easily.

In summary, ditch the reel, never allow any slack, play them close, and expect to land about 80 percent of your hook sets (short strikes notwithstanding). Once you're good at it, that other 20 percent is where the hook point happens to catch the fish by chance. Sometimes it's not the most ideal spot, and you can't help that. User error should account for little or nothing, and occasionally your opponent just makes a good move. I'm never disappointed in that; it's what any worthwhile trout is supposed to do.

For the most part, I find a net is the best way to limit unsafe handling and return the fish with the least amount of harm. I use forceps to carefully remove the hook and then set the net back underwater for the fish to swim away. They nearly always do, but in the event one does not, stick around and make sure he does (especially where eagles are present). Keep him upright and make sure he is breathing and regaining his balance. Just don't be in a hurry. If you'll be patient, most will right themselves and swim off. The ones that don't were either kept out too long or are bleeding from being hooked in a bad spot. Again, it's the risk we all accept when tying on a fly.

Photographing your catch is OK, but your priority should be safe handling and release of the fish.

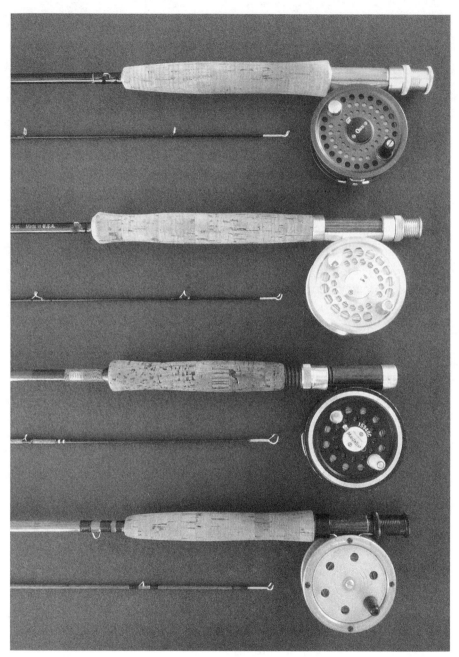

Weapons of choice: A timeless stillwater arsenal. Each rod and reel was modestly priced in its respective period and works just fine. Graphite rods are currently the norm (top two), while glass and bamboo were prevalent in years past (bottom two).

GEAR

Here I'll comment on my own preferences for stillwater fly fishing. I'm not much of a gear hound, but I'll tell you what I know. And take it with a big grain of salt, since better gear really won't help you locate, hook, or land more fish. Moreover, I wouldn't be in a hurry to have all this stuff at once; picking it up one piece at a time is more fun anyway.

Rod. I suppose any discussion related to fishing gear should begin with the rod, so we'll start there. Modern rods are made of graphite; fiberglass and bamboo were prevalent in the past. Graphite is certainly superior as a material; however, I wouldn't rule out the other two in terms of effectiveness. Plenty of trout have been taken on them over the years. A 5-weight is about right for most lakes, and that's all I use. For what it's worth, I have a mid-range rod that works beautifully, and it's likely I'll never buy an upper-end model for stillwater. For me that money is not well spent, but others may differ in opinion. Nothing wrong either way. Do yourself a favor though, and at least choose a brand with a good return policy and life guarantee. Paying a few bucks for a plan that will repair or replace a broken rod

Two of a kind: Pat and Corky Johnson are living proof that fiberglass rods are deadly as ever.

each time is a good arrangement for both you and the maker, and if you're like me, you'll break yours regularly. One other tip: Use paraffin wax on all your ferrule connections. Your rod won't come apart nearly as often when in action, and you'll have an easier time breaking it down.

Fly Reel. The reel stores your line, and that's what it's good for on still-water. In terms of performance, there's no reason to splurge here. An expensive reel is fine, but that's just your personal preference; the fish won't care. For a 5-weight, I prefer the traditional small arbor models with exposed rim and pop-off spools. I don't palm the rim to play fish, but it's nice to have the extra control when you're peeling off line to cast. Disc or click drag—take your pick.

Waders. Here I've found the extra money is actually well spent. Again, take the time to research it for yourself. But if you ask me, spending a little more is worth it for what you get. I spend a lot of hours in mine, and quality matters. Fins are worth the extra money, as well. Without naming brands, if you make the jump from low-end to high-end you'll be glad you did. I've

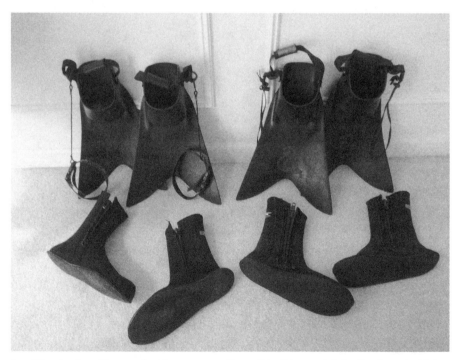

Anything to do with your feet is money well spent in this sport. I don't advocate high-end on most equipment, but you'll appreciate the difference when it comes to the maneuverability, comfort, and convenience afforded by good fins and footwear.

never heard anyone with upper-end fins say they were sorry for spending the money. Booties—I use them religiously. They allow you to walk around with fins off without wearing down the feet of your waders. Also, their comfort and maneuverability are superior to wading boots with fins. These are the neoprene zip-ups that have a thin sole on the bottom. Be careful with ones that have a rubberized toe box, as they can be too small on the inside or too big on the outside. Either is bad on your circulation. Mine have plenty of room in the toes, and I never need to wear thicker socks.

Line. A good line is also worth the extra cash. My suggestion is, if you're going to coin-up only once, this is the thing to spend on. I use a density-compensated Type V sinker almost exclusively, but we're all different. At the very least, be sure and have a fast, full sinker at the ready. One of the most common mistakes you'll see is someone showing up with a floater and slow sinker as an entire arsenal simply because, "I'm more comfortable with a floater and I have a sinker just in case!" By now you can see the problem with that.

Thermometer. Yes, and they're cheap.

Net. I like the rubber bagged versions now that weight is less of an issue. They're still on the heavy side, but upper-end models have gotten a

Standard magnets, brass hardware, and a length of shock cord make for an inexpensive yet effective way to store and use your net.

lot better. This is also money well spent if you plan to use yours often. I recommend a bow of at least 16 inches. I also rigged a good magnet and tether setup to my float tube, which allows easy access and storage of the net. A hint on magnets: Make sure all your hardware is nonmagnetic (i.e., brass), otherwise you'll see why.

Fly Box. I like the clear, double-sided ones that float and keep your flies dry. The inside sections are also interchangeable.

Forceps. Forceps also matter. I like mine compact, with a clamp and scissor option; nice ones will also have an eyelet poker.

Pack Straps. I like with my tube inflated, so these are essential. A good set of padded ones is inexpensive.

Leader/Tippet. Some prefer to go as light as possible for stealth. I find stealth is never an issue, but line strength sure is. Do yourself a favor and avoid chasing bigger fish while under-gunned. Most places I fish, I use 2X leader going to 3X tippet (fluorocarbon) underwater, and 3X going to 4X with drys. (Up to a size 16 fly you're generally OK using 4X tippet; any

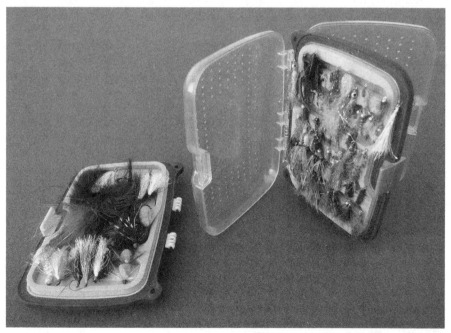

In the world of fly boxes, functional is not expensive, fancy is. Look for a sealed, floating version that allows good use of the space. I prefer a two-sided fly box with visibility from the outside. Some modern versions have interchangeable sections, which come in handy if the lakes freeze and one needs to go steelheading!

smaller and you'll need to size your tippet down, as tinier flies require a lesser diameter tippet to fit through the eyelet hole.) Pricing is all over the place; just avoid going too cheap.

Flies. Interestingly, I used fewer as a new fly fisher, evolved toward a much larger variety in time, and eventually moved back down to the small handful that I use today. My "less is more" approach to equipment certainly applies here. As always, this is another method that works for me and the style I have developed. Your preference may be for more variety, or simply a different set of patterns altogether. For reasons we have discussed, you have a lot of wiggle room when it comes to flies, so experiment and use what suits you best.

Spares and Extras. Spare equipment is also a smart idea, especially on long or far-away outings. Always avoid having to end a trip due to a broken rod. Spare rods, tips, and other essentials are worth the effort to bring them along. I always keep either a pack rod on my tube or a full spare in the truck. Spare reels are less important, but not a bad idea. (I've severed fly lines; it happens.) Leader, tippet, flies—all yes, and easy to pack along. Don't forget the patch kit for your float tube and waders. I have survived lots of trips in leaking waders, but an onsite patch kit takes up no space. Bring it. Beyond that, extra food, water, and TP should always come along (you'll thank me someday).

Two Rods. I don't carry two, but it's a matter of preference. Most serious stillwater guys opt for them to enable switching lines in an instant. I don't like carrying the second rod, and I tend to think twice about switching up because of losing that extra couple of minutes to swap spools. Using only one rod helps me think through decisions better; plus, if I switch out, I'll tend to commit more to the other method before switching back. In most cases, having only one rod pays off, since lack of action is usually not solved by something as simple as a fly or line change. If I'm getting beat, I'm forced to think about the bigger picture. But in the grand scale, I don't see either switching or not switching as a game maker. That means, do as you wish.

Boats and Other Watercraft. I'm a float-tube guy because it suits the methods and locations I fish most often. I don't travel over long stretches of water or fish big lakes, and I do prefer something highly maneuverable—in addition to something I can hike with. In general, a tube is more maneuverable while fishing, but a pontoon will get you more places faster. Beyond that, we all have different needs and preferences, so my advice is take your time researching before buying anything.

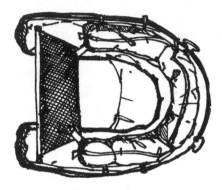

You have no shortage of options when it comes to suitable watercraft. Many fly fishers gravitate toward a float tube when versatility and maneuverability on the water, as well as portability and ease of storage off the water, are major considerations.

More on watercraft: By and large, you'll do a lake the most justice by floating it if a fly rod is your weapon of choice. In many cases, the shoreline is either inaccessible or nearly impossible to cast a fly from. (Note that there are exceptions here. For example, many of the stillwater venues found throughout the United Kingdom come to mind. These fisheries are often designed and groomed to accommodate presentation from shore or land.)

When hiking in is part of the equation, a float tube is generally best. Again, you have lots of options, and here you'll want to consider weight and transportability among other characteristics. In general, U- and V-shaped tubes are safer and easier to launch; these are the obvious choice for more full-bodied anglers. The O-shaped tubes are lightweight and highly maneuverable; however, they require more skill to launch in rough terrain and tend to have a lower weight capacity. Anglers weighing over 200 pounds are better served in a U or V boat. Most pontoons are not suitable options for hiking due to size and weight issues. Inflatable rafts usually fall somewhere in the middle; anglers use them and they work. A few pack-specific boat designs have been developed, as well. If those interest you, do your homework and make sure your money is well spent.

Do yourself a big favor, and prioritize a floating device right up there with your rod and reel. For the most part, this is the only effective way to cover all the water available to you in an outing. Without a floating device, you can seldom place yourself where fish are located. There is no shortage of options when it comes to suitable watercraft, but most fly anglers gravitate toward a float tube, pontoon, or pram. Versatility and maneuverability

Adam Carroll enjoys a scenic mountain pond while outplaying one of its feisty cutthroat.

on the water—as well as portability and storability off the water—are among the major considerations. Note: Life preservers are mandatory in boats and pontoons; float tubes are usually exempt from this requirement, but use good judgment.

When transporting anything inflatable, watch your air pressure, because elevation or warmth can send it through the roof. I've had one blowout from over-inflation, and that was more than enough. Warm weather caused the tube to expand, and the outer shell gave way at the inner seam where the seat attaches at one side. Within seconds, the shell ripped out on the left side as the bladder stretched inward over my lap. Before it could rupture, I let some air out of the bladder while heading for shore. In 50-degree water, I was just grateful the shell gave way first and I didn't have to go swimming.

Hiking with a float tube and fly gear: If you keep your float tube inflated, shed a little air before going up into elevation, and keep a little squish in it all day. I find it's easier and more time-efficient to leave all the air in when hiking up. With my hour limit on distance, I'm generally not going far enough to warrant packing a deflated tube. You can also ditch the backpack and use the tube itself to store and carry gear. It's surprising how well this works on shorter hikes. If you have more items than can be packed onto a float tube, I'd rethink the amount of stuff you're bringing along. I always have everything I need, and it always fits easily. That includes all gear, waders, fins, net, extra layers, food, fluids—literally everything. For air, I just bring the hose and leave my pump at the truck. I seldom need to add much air, so lung power is plenty. For those who would rather carry a pump, some good, compact options are easily found. Finally, a good set of padded pack-straps for the tube is essential. Your local fly shop is a good bet for these.

Waders, pack or wear? On most hikes you're best to pack them. With neoprene waders, I would advise doing this every time. If you own breath-

Example of a fully loaded float tube: Rear compartment holds waders, booties, spare pack rod, and miscellaneous odds and ends; left side holds food, water, and coffee; right side holds all fly tackle and dry thermals. Tucked beneath the apron are my net, fins, jackets, and hat. Attached to the other side, or bottom, are the pack straps. On most trips I'll carry the rod fully rigged, since I have two free hands.

able waders, you'll find it easier to wear them in, if the walk is a short one. Some of the ponds I frequent can be reached in a few minutes, and I find it a lot easier to put on and take off my waders at the truck. However, beyond a 20-minute hike, I'd opt to pack them in. Use the same rule of thumb for booties if you have them. They're OK for a short walk on easy terrain, but the soles won't hold up for anything more.

Other Gear and Clothing. This is the time to grab those spare rods and fly lines and see how they're working. When exploring a new pond, or fishing a familiar one with a lot of structure (and that's most of them), you're smart to leave your Sunday best at home. Rest assured that you're already going to lose flies out there, and your lines will likely take some abuse. And for some mysterious reason, rods tend to be more fragile in these settings. I find it best to take my old stuff and bring a second rod along as backup. If you only have two rods, use your good one as the spare this time.

Clothing can be a trick with the limited space you have. At the very least bring rain gear. And if you're like me, you'll break a sweat getting most places. Usually a synthetic inner layer will do the trick, but I might

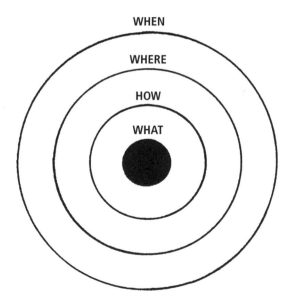

WHEN-WHERE-HOW-WHAT. Your search will be most effective when prioritized in this order. Start with timing (WHEN) and drill down to location (WHERE). Then, based on response, dial in the best method (HOW). Your choice of fly (WHAT) will provide any fine-tuning, if any is needed. Much of the time, the first three will be all it takes.

also bring an extra shirt and change out. If you're soaked by the time you get there, you don't want to stay that way for long. Ditch the wet clothing and start over. I usually hang mine on a branch to dry while I fish.

Miscellaneous Advice. Just as golfers keep their clubs in the trunk, I always recommend keeping your stuff at the ready to the extent that it's secure. My more valuable gear stays in the house, but anything else that I usually take always stays in the truck. I think it's best to keep a duffel bag loaded with rain gear, extra layers, hats, gloves, and such. That way, regardless of the season, it's all right there. Better still, have your lakeside routine down to a science so you won't waste valuable time between showing up and getting in. With time often so limited, a handful of those little things can add up and start to matter.

I hope all this WHEN–WHERE–HOW–WHAT stuff has been useful. It works best in that order, and it is the most effective way I have found to organize and make sense of all those invaluable small details. The good news is we've now covered the basic important steps of finding, fooling, and capturing trout on our lakes and ponds. Going forward, we'll apply these principles in different scenarios and see what happens.

Lesson 4

DISSECTING A LAKE

It wasn't exactly the best of times. Subprime lending had taken a skid, world markets had crashed, and economies everywhere were underwater. As an unemployed finance professional, I did what anyone should in the face of such turmoil and uncertainty: I went fishing. And I fished a lot. As the days went on, I had the good fortune of spending an abundance of time at Pass Lake in the northwest corner of Washington State. Before long this habit became an addiction, and then the addiction spun out of control.

I was not only learning the more subtle secrets of this body of water, I was also getting an Ivy-League education in the finer points of stillwater fly fishing. Soon my friends and neighbors began to take notice and make mention of it. Some might otherwise call it "making fun." One thing led to another and, the next I knew, the lake was being referred to as my office. I knew then that I needed help. Eventually I rejoined the work force, thus ending the binge. However, the reference to *my office* stuck. So I offer this use of the term to benefit all those who find the need to take refuge at this kind of special place—while not blowing their cover at home. For example: "Honey I'm afraid I'll be home late tonight . . . I have to stay late at the office," or "Sorry I missed your birthday, Timmy . . . I just couldn't break free from the office . . . I'm sure you understand!" The list goes on. So remember, you can have an *office* within reasonable commute and still be home in time to tuck the kids in.

For any serious stillwater fly fisher, having a home court and knowing it inside and out are essential to developing the better part of one's game. Beyond the study of one particular sample in Washington, this lesson demonstrates how to dissect any lake, and most importantly, *your* lake.

89

Here we'll look closely at Pass Lake and pick apart how and why it produces so consistently. Moreover, we'll look at how to bury the hook more often there—or anywhere else.

So why Pass? It's not the closest lake for most in the area, a state highway runs right alongside parts of it, and there's often jet noise from the nearby naval air station. We established earlier that there is no such thing as the perfect lake setting, and Pass certainly supports that. But as a home court, this 99-acre venue offers a level of sport that baffles beginners and provides a hardy challenge, time and time again, to even the most experienced veterans. A classic stillwater angler's lake, Pass has the trout population, food variety, climate, and terrain that create the ultimate puzzle in a constant state of flux. And with the advantages of catch-and-release fly-fishing-only regulations, and a year-round season, the lake is unsurpassed among lowland stillwater in western Washington.

FISH POPULATION

At present, the lake holds an impressive stock of rainbows, along with a supply of brown trout that is among the best in the region. Pass also holds

This overweight rainbow was not about to say no to an "unsuspecting" leech. The lake regularly holds a crop of these older trout, and fish exceeding 20 inches can be commonplace at certain times.

a few pumpkinseed *(Lepomis gibbosus)* that do not show often. I've only taken three or four of them in the recent past. The lake has been reported to hold other species in its history—tiger trout, cutthroat, and Atlantic salmon among them. On the whole, rainbows tend to outnumber browns by about five to one; however, on any given day you may see nothing but rainbows. Or, at the right time, an unusually high ratio of browns might come calling. I've never had a day of all browns that I can recall, but I've come close. Over time, the lake tends to support generations in all sizes for both rainbows and browns. Both grow faster than average and regularly reach sizes over 20 inches. The lake has much larger fish, but sightings become scarce beyond 22 or 23 inches. On average, the majority of both species caught are in the 14- to 18-inch range.

Pass is in a unique marine climate that allows favorable year-round conditions along with a good variety of abundant food sources, but here's the real reason for quality of stocks: regulations. It still amazes me that, given the sheer number of lakes in the region, so few are designated as catch-and-release, or restricted. Look at any of the few that are, and the evidence supporting this policy is overwhelming. But that's a whole other discussion.

Although rare, pumpkinseed will make an occasional cameo in warmer months. In countless hours on Pass Lake, I've managed to catch three of them.

SEASONS AND WEATHER

Having the lake so close to Deception Pass, a major saltwater passage, allows the local marine climate to provide better-than-average year-round conditions, which often means cooler weather in summer and the opposite in winter. In general, Pass is one of the last lakes to hit undesirable warm temperatures or to ice over. It still does both, but, overall, the lake will provide more fishable days during the year than most others on average. Put another way, Pass might be unfishable a very small part of the year, if at all. I define the fishable range at Pass to be anything not frozen up to about 72 degrees F at surface. A temperature of 72 degrees sounds warm, but at Pass it takes extreme hot weather to affect the surface because of its location.

The lake also has reasonable depth, which provides much cooler layering underneath at any given time. In my experience, fish have held lower down in these conditions and, when hooked, still have had a surprising amount of energy.

Additionally, the one time I observed Pass to actually reach 72 degrees at surface, the spike was very short-lived; the lower layers never had the chance to heat up much. We just don't have the extreme weather to sustain those uncomfortable temperatures out there. That said, when it's above 70 degrees or so at surface, or whenever the fish display lower energy levels, it is good practice to just stay off the water and give them a break. And to be clear, I don't mean to say 72 degrees is an acceptable temperature in all circumstances. How long the temperature remains at that level, and the energy levels displayed in the fish, are factors to consider as well. In a different scenario, 68 degrees might be unacceptable. It's a simple matter of using good judgment.

Even when ice forms, the lake can remain partially unfrozen, as the sun that time of year cuts a nice line through the second bay toward the point. When the launch area is under solid ice, Bay #2 can be accessed from roadside; anyone who hits it right can have the bay and the entire point across from it to himself. Even in freezing temperatures, a sunny morning or afternoon will bring some action up. Be aware of the risk when ice is present. Always fish with a partner, watch daytime temperatures, and don't stick around for the sun to disappear.

By having more mild conditions than average, Pass also tends to have more favorable water temperatures. For this and other reasons mentioned, fishing is among the best in Washington stillwaters. However, don't expect the weather at Pass to match your neighborhood. Though it tends to be warmer than the temperature at home most days, I've seen it go both ways; always be prepared to layer up or down when you arrive. Surprisingly, winds are calmer than I would expect for a location surrounded by salt water, but the land immediately around Pass provides a good buffer. Most days the wind comes in from the direction of Deception Pass Bridge, so it blows from the launch, past the point, and toward the far end. This has implications for locating fish; we'll get to that.

Overall, spring and fall are best, because they happen to coincide with ideal temperatures and some of the better food sources. Beyond that, the lake provides good action any time of year—short of when it's icing over. Most success will be had from paying attention to current conditions rather than simply considering what month it may be.

PEA SOUP AT PASS

The lake has a reputation for serving up this popular menu item, particularly in fall. Unattractive as it is, algae tends to deter anglers more than it does fish. If anything, I have found the green slime to enhance the bite. It acts just like surface chop or overcast in terms of limiting surface visibility, so the fish tend to be less bashful about coming up to feed; they aren't as visible in the water. From the angler's perspective, clarity remains pretty good down through the layers. Anything that limits transparency at surface while still allowing good visibility underneath helps create conditions for good fishing.

FOOD SOURCES

Pass is rich in a variety of food sources throughout the year. My purpose here is to provide as much useful information as I can about the lake outside of time-bound constraints. To that end—at Pass or any lake—food sources will cycle differently year to year; no two years are ever alike. You'll recall we discussed that previously.

Minnows. Perhaps the primary source for fattening up so many fish, Pass's minnow population is known to provide food for most or all of the year. When trout are grouped along shore, minnows often are the reason. When minnows are packed along the bank, you can often spot them "dancing around" at the surface. Whenever that happens, you can be certain the fish aren't far away. It's usually only a matter of time before fish can be seen taking them as the minnows create all that disturbance.

Our previous discussion on minnows fully applies here. Where minnows are concentrated in-tight, the fish will likely accept your offerings early in the feed cycle then start to ignore you when the same spot has been active for several days or more. The feed may continue for some time, and your best bet will be to work the surrounding open area. The fish will be less bashful out there and, though a number of minnows will have ventured out into the open, your fly still stands a better chance there than among all that competition along the bank. In simpler terms, explore your options and don't waste a lot of time where fish just aren't interested in your presentation, even where concentrations are visible. There's nothing wrong with ignoring all that excitement and going instead for something you can't see.

Regarding fly selection, you don't always have to match minnows exactly. Consider visibility and how aggressive (or not) the trout appear to be. I stay with the smaller leech pattern about half the time. If you ask me, due to its profile, a leech makes a pretty good small minnow—and most trout seem to agree. A Mickey Finn or similar pattern is also a nice alternative, and I don't find color to be a big determining factor.

Midges. If anything can match the prolific presence of minnows at Pass, it's these. If you can't see them breaking the surface and taking flight, let the swallows lead the way. For much of the year, these smallish, agile birds will swarm the surface at Pass, sometimes on and off throughout the day. They make a great indicator for midge activity. However, you may or may not find trout feeding on active midges. In my observation, midges can occur so frequently that trout may ignore them at times in favor of other available foods. With midges, it seems to work like that bowl of pretzels on your counter. They'll do in a pinch, but during a full-course meal, they're the last thing you'd turn to.

On one of my outings, midges were very fishable for maybe three or four weeks out and to the right of the launch. I could just join the swarm of swallows and start casting. The action was a lot of fun for several outings, and then the fish began to disappear, even though the midges (and swallows) continued on. What happened was minnows started coming in around the point. The fish knew early-on to shift to the next food source. Trout are well known for looking ahead and adjusting to the next food occurrence, even when the existing source is still the most prolific. In terms of method, I'm not one to match Chironomids at Pass. I have more fun tempting fish with a larger, more aggressive, offering in the face of so much

Dinner is served: A staple in the diet of any Pass Lake inhabitant, the midge occurs year-round and has a reputation for intense hatch activity at times.

activity. However, the lake always draws a notable crowd of Chironomid fishers when midges are abundant. Those proficient at it enjoy very good success at Pass.

Callibaetis. My personal favorite at Pass. Of all the foods that occur there, this one is fished best when matched. During spring, look for *Callibaetis* over the shoals where vegetation grows, and expect hatches to go off for up to several weeks. The *Callibaetis* hatch at Pass tends to be the first good indicator of the year about how the lake's older fish have fared over the winter. In the weeks before this hatch, most of the active fish are the younger generation, typically rainbows, that feed heavily on the first good midge hatch since the cold of winter.

It's worth keeping in mind that the *Callibaetis* hatch can show a lot differently from year to year, more so than other food sources. In a strong year, *Callibaetis* will come up week after week, averaging size 12 or so early on, and it will seem as if the entire fish population has reservations at the table. In fact, all day before and after the hatch, there can be hardly a fish to be had. But as it goes off, there will be action everywhere along the shoals. Even before the first visible signs, there are fish to be had underwater on nymphs, maybe for an hour or so. Then, when surface breaks, there are fish everywhere, feeding with reckless abandon, both rainbows and browns.

And size is not an issue; they all want in on it. This is the kind of dry fly fishing you'd pay a lot of money and travel a long way to find, and it's here right in our back yard. There is no way of knowing what the *Callibaetis* hatch will be like each spring, but even when it's only half as good as it could be, it's worth skipping work for. Timing tip: Pass Lake is located in Skagit County, home to the world's largest tulip crop. When Skagit's tulips first pop for spring, think of the *Callibaetis* hatch at Pass. The two tend to be nicely correlated each year; when one begins to show, so does the other. They both seem to require that same spring warm-up before coming out.

In general the *Callibaetis* hatch starts off very strong, impressive in both size and numbers. The hatch will vary each day in time and duration, depending on weather and water conditions. Most days, it starts late morning to early afternoon, and lasts anywhere from an hour to about two and a half hours. Over time the hatch slowly weakens, with the bugs becoming smaller. Though it also fluctuates throughout the cycle, the bite eventually peters out as fish start the shift to the next major source.

In terms of tactics, you'll first need to find and recognize the hatch. Usually the sudden burst of overwhelming rises will be the big tip-off. It happens simultaneously with the surface break, so the splashing is always

Unable to take flight, this cripple had just enough time to pose for me before retiring as fish food.

An emerger and a little patience were enough to take this brown during a *Callibaetis* hatch. If you enjoy seeing the lake's oldest browns rise to a dry fly, this hatch is the time to go fishing.

noticeable before the onslaught of oversized mayflies. Once you dial it in, the sight of all this is more than impressive; try to keep your hat on straight.

Now that we've established the jackpot and placed you directly in the middle of it, the game is mostly about good hook sets. At times you'll follow the rises, but in general they'll follow you. On the take, you'll need that short hesitation and a soft lift. It won't require much, and there is no issue with lodging the point of the hook, so the most common mistake is reacting too fast and pulling back too hard. Not to worry; the results will force you to figure it out. And you'll get plenty of practice, as these fish mean business and are anything but shy. That hatch only goes a short time each day, and the fish know it, so they'll keep scarfing down until dinner is no longer served. On any good hook set, remember to keep the pressure on; don't get timid just because that hook is only a #16. The main thing is, don't get discouraged by all the missed strikes. Just have fun playing the game, and enough of them will find their way to your net. This kind of action doesn't happen nearly enough, so let go of the landing fetish for once and enjoy all the chaos. For what it's worth, I've landed as few as 5 and as many as 19 by doing the same thing, in the same situation, for the same amount of time. *Callibaetis* hatches are like that.

Bug-wise, I prefer a good emerger, as a lot of times the fish will stay low, rolling and sipping, and a standard dry pattern can be tough to lodge. They'll readily take either, so do yourself a favor and keep a stash of emergers on hand, as they stick to nearly anything. Last tip, inspect your fly often and be prepared to change it out more than normal. Flies tend to get bent or chewed up easily in this situation, and you can unknowingly waste 10 or 20 minutes using a bum fly. That's forever in one of these hatches.

Damsels. These are like a lot of anglers I know: They only show up in fair weather. Look for them late spring through early fall at Pass. Midday through afternoon on a nice day is usually busiest. On an active day they will concentrate against the shoreline, but they can be seen all across the lake. Besides minnows, damsels are about the only prey that can bring otherwise wary trout into the shallows in broad daylight during the heat of an afternoon. This is a prime example of trout going against their better judgment in favor of fine dining. When you spot damsels against shore like that, assume fish are on them, whether you see anything or not. Maybe half the time, trout are actually visible when feeding on damsels. It depends mostly on depth and terrain. Whether the fish are visible or not, keep in mind that they prefer to chase the nymphs as they run up toward shore from a few yards out. Hate to say it again, but leeches and other lake flies will produce every bit as well as a damsel nymph pattern. Take your pick.

Caddis. I'm mentioning these for good measure, since they are officially part of the menu at Pass. However, if I went on about how and where they occur, and how to fish them like an expert, I'd be pulling your leg. They are there, and I have seen them—but that's where the story ends. I have yet to spend time getting good with caddis flies at Pass. Then again, there was a day when I would have said that about *Callibaetis*. Hopefully it's a matter of time, and one day I'll find myself smack in the middle of a good binge.

Crayfish. Another year-round dweller. Tough to say how much of a trout's diet these make up, but Pass has a very good population of them. And like the fish, they can grow surprisingly large. My best guess is, the younger ones feed older trout. I don't imitate crayfish directly; however, when browns inhabit rocky sections of shoreline, these have to be the preferred fare at times. Logically, to me, any fish patrolling the banks for crayfish would be hard-pressed to say *no* to a nice leech or minnow that happens by. As for actual crayfish patterns, I've seen some impressive ones

A healthy and balanced ecosystem yields good-size crayfish at Pass Lake. Locals have done well catching them when the season is open, and small baited traps are the mainstay.

as of late. In my opinion, they'll work as well as anything—but not any better. If you like it, use it.

A final word on hatches and such: It's great to figure them out and make a match with your fly, and many would even define the sport that way. That's not wrong; in fact it can be a lot of fun. But beyond that, I think there is tremendous value in understanding which factors actually matter in drawing strikes, and which are indifferent. It has everything to do with understanding your prey. In my experience, the best results come from simply finding the food source and, first, discerning if fish are onto it. Then if they are, discerning where they are located and how they are moving and feeding. From there, a good approach and presentation are chosen and executed. Get that far and you're 99 percent there, before fly selection ever comes into play. And in most cases, it may not. A good fly fisher understands when matching is important, when it's likely not, and when thinking outside the box is a more prudent move.

Some of my own favorites at Pass Lake: Beadhead Simi Seal Leech, Bullethead Minnow, Damsel Nymph, Callibaetis Emerger. Perhaps the best tip on fly selection at Pass is to think twice before sizing up. The lake has a good population of larger trout; however, an oversized presentation is rarely the most effective way to fish for them. Always consider visibility and other factors.

LAYOUT

At 99 acres, Pass can easily be covered in a single outing, even from a float tube. Maximum depth is about 20 feet. The major inlet is located at the far roadside corner, while the major outlet can be found near the boat launch. Neither tends to be a hotbed for holding fish and, though I've taken my share near both, more significant factors could be cited for that. Highway 20 runs along the south shoreline, bordering the first bay out from the boat launch and rejoining the lake at Bay #2. The opposite shore runs along the old orchard and park ranger's quarters (Pass is located within the boundaries of Deception Pass State Park). The lake has just enough depth, cover, and surrounding buffers, along with that marine climate, to keep its inhabitants comfortable throughout the year. The shoal off the point (left from the launch and across from Bay #2) extends out midway across toward the road. The shoal drop-off is more abrupt on the right side of the point than the left; when I'm on the water, I think of this shoal as skewed left. The way it fishes generally supports that. The entire far end is one big shoal, all the way from the road to the orchard. Again, that's exactly how it fishes. By day I prefer to fish the far end, given the sheer acreage of that far shoal, as compared to the point. The point is a much smaller area and can be good in the evening simply for its convenient location at quitting time. That matters in a float tube.

Beyond its shoals, Pass also boasts some of the best shoreline terrain anywhere. The entire lake is lined with a variety of cover, ranging from

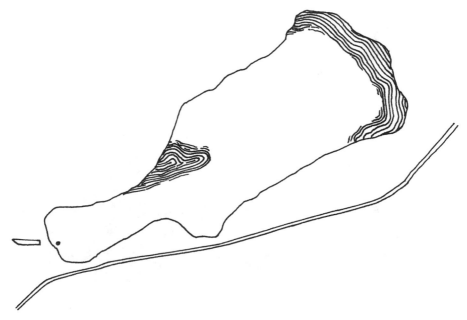

Pass Lake in the northwest corner of Washington State. The lake has two major shoal areas: the point and the far end. The point is nearest to the boat launch and provides a convenient and often productive area to work in, while the far end boasts a more widespread shallow section that is generally less pressured. When time allows, visiting the far end is usually worth the trip. The remaining shorelines provide good to excellent fish cover that features overhang, fallen trees, and rock structure. Special regulations that include catch-and-release fly fishing only, and a requirement for all watercraft to be self-propelled, have created one of the premier quality fisheries in the region.

shallow weeds to rock structure to thick overhang. Throughout much of the day, you can find good stretches of shade. Like most, I have my preferred sections of shoreline at Pass, but to say any of it is better than the rest would be misleading. As you can guess by now, any number of factors will have fish gathered in different parts of the shoreline at a given time. And often you won't find squat near shore, no matter where you choose to patrol.

Other considerations with terrain include structure, drop-offs, and even wind direction at times. Pass isn't known for a lot of debris to hang up on along the bottom, although it has plenty. The amount of debris in a lake is relative. I've seen a lot worse in other places, and Pass is pretty tame in comparison. Overall, you won't have to spend much time trying to unwrap yourself or free flies from sunken trees and the like; however, novice casters will spend some time unsnagging from shoreline debris. Regarding drop-offs and the lake bottom, I don't find it's a big game changer here. At times I'll treat the area right off the point as a legitimate drop-off. I will work

Perhaps the deepest, and certainly most abrupt, section of shoreline at Pass, this rock structure does not always hold fish. But when it does, a skilled angler can have a field day.

The Orchard has prime trout water, complete with an oversized shoal that extends out beyond the small bay. This area of the lake also boasts a weedy shoreline, along with a variety of treed structure and a small point.

parts of the shoreline for deeper cover when the drop is abrupt, but that's about it. I haven't found that kind of placement to affect much at Pass as it might elsewhere.

WIND AT PASS

Wind direction will matter at times, either with respect to food location or reduction in visibility. Since the wind usually blows from the launch toward the far end, feeding can be enhanced just beyond the point (to the right), and toward shore at the far end, as food and debris are sometimes carried to those areas. When feeding is present in shallow depths, always consider the various surface textures caused by wind. Surface chop, artificial seams, and any other disturbance created by moving air are all worth investigating. But by far the most significant effect wind can have at Pass is along the shoreline. In stronger winds, the unprotected side of the lake can become a hotbed of holding and feeding fish. Consider the instant influx of food and

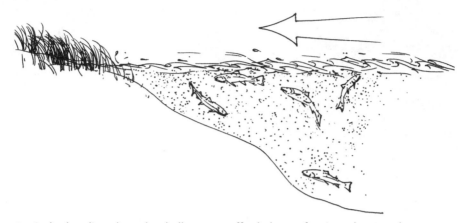

A windy shoreline along the shallows can afford plenty of action when rough water stirs up food and limited surface visibility allows fish added cover. Regardless of the advantages, always play it safe in rough conditions and opt out when in question.

debris that suddenly inundates the bank, along with the safe-haven created by reduced visibility from all that choppy water as it slaps against shore. Intuitively, we tend to work the opposite side, where conditions are calm; however, this only caters to our own comfort and convenience, and not much else. For anyone willing to combat the wind and chop, the windy-side shoreline can afford unbelievable results at times.

In an extreme example from my own experience, I arrived at Pass the Saturday before Thanksgiving one year, only to find temperatures in the mid-30s and high winds from a recent system that had blown in from the north. Bellingham had received a surprise snow the night before, and it seemed Pass was just inside the southern tip of that system. The lake was completely void of anglers, and at first I sat there contemplating whether to even get out of the truck. As I watched the mini-whitecaps blow across the lake, I noticed the direction of the wind was off its normal routine; it was blowing from the house toward the highway. Two thoughts occurred to me: One, I had driven an hour to get up here; and two, I had seen in the past what high winds could do to stack fish along the receiving shoreline. Furthermore, the water was still over 50 degrees, so these cold winds weren't going to mean anything to the fish. I also knew that my tube would be all over the place, and casting would be anything but fun. I added it all up and decided to get in and give it the 15-minute test. Two things proved out: For one, as I had suspected, it was a struggle out there. For the other, as I had hoped, the shoreline was loaded. When I approached the far end, the wind was softer, and, sure enough, the action was noticeably slower. So instead of continuing around toward the house, I reversed direction and worked the same route back toward the truck. Sure enough, as I got back into the windier area, the action sped up again. In three and a half hours the road-side shoreline from Bay #2 to the far end coughed up 44 fish, with another six to eight lost, and about a dozen missed strikes. Collectively, that's over 60 strikes—every one of them right against shore—and most were the larger rainbows. My only regret was not showing up till 1 p.m. that day.

Obviously a windy shoreline won't guarantee action, but I never ignore the circumstance. The potential is too great, and if the fish are in, I'll gladly put up with all that rough water. Note: A tube is likely your only option in windier conditions. But if the water is just too rough to maneuver safely, don't even consider going in. It's not worth it.

Eight days later, the surface had cooled by 10 degrees from the arctic blast that week. Again I fished the afternoon, but, for two straight hours of hard work in 42-degree water, I only managed to land eight fish. Still a pretty good take, but barely a fraction of the previous weekend when temperatures were warmer and those high winds pushed all food and fish to the roadside shoreline. These two scenarios nicely illustrate the wide variety of effects different conditions can have on Pass. When an angler pays attention and responds to a day's circumstances, anything can happen.

METHODS

I'll keep it general this time, as I've hit the subject pretty hard already. By now it's no secret I prefer to locate fish that are grouped for a specific purpose and then use a fairly universal approach and fly to draw out as many of them as I can. I keep a very simple arsenal as well, most often a 5-weight rod and reel with Type V full-sink line and 3X fluorocarbon for tippet. It works everywhere from the shoreline to the open water, from near-surface to the depths, around cover and back again. A popular variation of the fly is using a minnow or similar streamer pattern, particularly to work the shore-line. Time it right, and this is some of the best fun you can have out there.

Once again, when working the bank, keep your boat out and away, square up like in basketball, and take your shot straight in. You have plenty of options in terms of depth, retrieve, and such when working along shore. Try a bit of everything, as it's good to experiment. I usually lay casts two to three yards apart if I'm making my way along, depending on how the cover lays out. Some anglers prefer to be closer together, and there is nothing

Pass Lake has a very good variety of shoreline cover. Shallow weedy sections, fallen trees, and rock structures are all abundant and provide plenty of action at times.

Certain conditions can reduce visibility and thereby act like structure. Rain and fog are prime examples, and Pass' marine climate provides plenty of both.

wrong with that. My theory of method takes field-of-vision into account and assumes there can be too much of a good thing, meaning too many casts within the sight of a single fish is counterproductive, but I'll admit it's a theory. Another good trick is "backstitching," or turning back and re-casting where you've already passed. If you have an indication that fish are there, this can be effective. Some fish may be on the move, or one of your previous casts may have been noticed but not pursued. Another good shoreline practice is to make subsequent passes through an area that shows well in terms of strikes. For whatever reason, fish can, at times, be stacked in one particular stretch.

Try and get in the habit of picturing the scene underwater. With very few clues, you can visualize a great deal and, from there, draw conclusions that influence your decisions as you go along. Sounds simplistic, but with some experience you'll start recognizing game-changing events that would have gone unnoticed before.

When working the shoals at Pass, I prefer to section them off—once again using a cast-pause-strip-repeat approach. Short of obvious signs of food or fish, I'll methodically search each of three sections: the outer shoal near surface, the outer shoal at depth, and the shoreline. I give each a good

Ripe for the picking: Working the shoreline along the orchard. Note the shallow weeds, windy conditions, and blackish water from the day's thick overcast. Not the most scenic day by far, but when it means exceptional fishing, I can get over it.

About 70 yards left of the rock face, the Green Wall is a thick section of treed over-hang that provides a nice underwater shelter where even the largest trout can hold and feed. Cast right up against, count it down, start stripping, and hang on. The "Wall" held fish on this particular day.

scrub before moving on. I'd say 30 minutes, tops, will tell me if anything is active along a shoal, and that's probably generous. I'll usually give the point only 10 to 15 minutes, given its smaller size. If it has any activity, the first strike can easily be found in that amount of time. For what it's worth, the majority of fish I take at Pass are found on or near the shoals. Keep the shallow depths of a shoal in mind as you work through. I see a lot of anglers placing their bodies where their casts should be, and running float tubes or pontoons right over the top of prime holding water. If you're going in blind (that's most of the time), start with the outer parts first and then work in toward shore if no strikes. Much as you would with the shore-line, stay out beyond the outer shoal and cast inward. There may only be a few feet of water between surface and the top of the vegetation, and you'll want your fly there first before 300 pounds of man and machine come barreling through.

Matteo Michi (left) and Roy Spradlin work the far end shoal in Roy's "P-40."

Speaking of vegetation, Pass is famous for providing a different hedge footprint each year. Since the lake is so rich in vegetation, each season's set of unique conditions will determine where and how much the vegetation will come in when the warmer months arrive. That means your shoals will lay out differently every year and, just like with shifting river sections, you'll have to relearn the cover each season. Hint: Big numbers of fish will hold and feed around this shifting vegetation. I'm spelling it out because paying attention to the hedge configuration can yield great rewards. Many of the fish I take from the shoals at Pass came out from around these hedges. Treat hedges like any other structure, because that's exactly what they are. Sadly, most folks run right over them in pursuit of the "good spots." I'd love to know how many well placed, catchable fish I ignorantly run over in a day, compared to how many I actually take. (Or maybe I don't want to know.)

For all these reasons, the best thing you can do when fishing a shoal is to develop a sense of vision below the surface. It matters here even more than along the shoreline. Once you can picture the contours of the lake bottom, how the vegetation lays out, and where any structure is, you can start

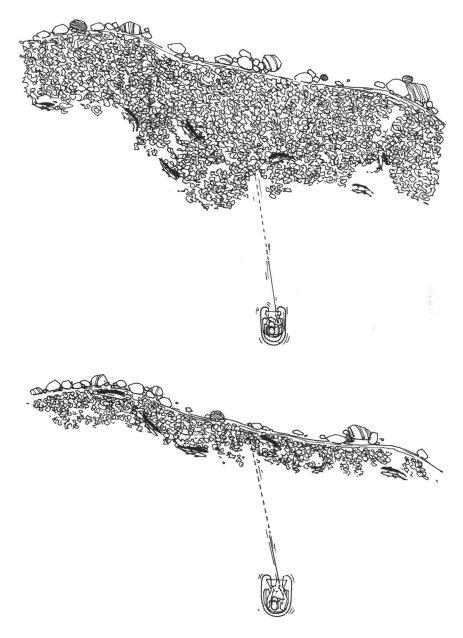

Underwater vegetation or hedges often shift from year to year, given the changing conditions in the surrounding environment. A hedge that one year extends several yards out from shore (top) may retract to within a few feet the following year (bottom), requiring an angler to learn all new positions when working the same section of shallows.

determining where fish are most likely positioned—then identify where their field of vision probably is. Eventually you can develop that sense for the entire lake, being able to "see" underwater and relate a very limited number of clues to the most likely scenario of fish activity. At Pass, so much goes on unseen to the eye. You can watch a guy repeatedly hit fish in what appears to be no-man's land, unable to tell where all his luck is coming from. Imagine your own luck and the unbelievable payoff when you've developed that sense of vision.

In open water I search and work through groups of fish the same as I would along shoals, using the same cast-pause-strip-repeat routine. Some tips on covering open water at Pass: When fish are visible near the surface, keep your presentation between you and them, meaning don't go over the top of them and hope to drag it back by for a strike. In my experience at Pass, since many of those fish are older and cautious, you can say goodbye the moment that big, clunky fly line slaps against their dorsal. And in the right circumstance, you can watch eight or ten of them scramble off together as your line splashes down. It's glorious. As always, put it down soft in their field of vision, short stunned pause, and then rip it back. If you do it right, they'll chase anything.

In the absence of visible fish, I usually blind-search in a logical pattern of movement until I get action. For me, that means casting in a circle from one position, as if cutting a pie. If I have high hopes, the pie has maybe

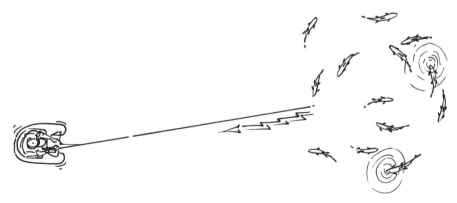

Sight-casting in open water can require a fair amount of finesse. Place your fly reasonably short of any observed activity, thereby avoiding an unnatural or threatening presentation. Then retrieve back and away. When you cast directly over any fish near the surface, your fly line will likely send them running.

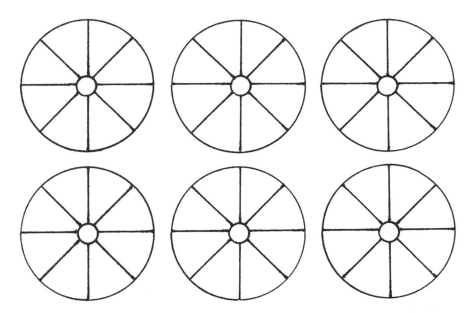

When covering a broad area of open water, use the pie method. You're at the center of each circle, and each slice of the pie represents a cast. Each circle of casts is a rotation, or full pie. Your area is covered most efficiently when several pies are grouped closely together without overlapping. Truth be told, I take a lot of shortcuts when it comes to actual execution—I'll do some variation each time without ever running the full drill. It's a lot of casting and movement, and I can determine how active an area is well before completing a sequence like this. Use it as a starting point for covering open water, and then develop your own preference as you gain experience.

eight slices. If my expectations are lower, I'll hold it to four or so. And varying the depth on retrieves is entirely within reason. After each complete circle, I'll move far enough to do another one—covering all new water. I'll do this again and again until I've covered a good sample of the area. Usually that's four to six circles—which doesn't sound like much, but try it next time you go out. A circle of casts around you covers more area than you realize. Besides that, a small handful of these circles will be enough to determine if fish are present. If something hits during a circle of casts, I'll immediately start concentrating on that location, attempting to "follow the strikes" and turn one into more. If you assume fish are social and that finding one will lead to his friends, you can keep drawing a line from one fish to the next, based on the location of strikes. So when things go right, that pattern of circles shouldn't last long anyway.

Beyond that, there are probably a hundred good options for covering open water. Mine is easy for my brain to follow, and it works if the fish are there. Anything that satisfies those two criteria for you is a good choice. At Pass, a good number of nice-size fish will patrol the open areas just below surface a lot of the time. I suspect this is truer at Pass than in other lakes, simply because Pass has more and your average put-and-take doesn't even come close to supporting the same number of older generations. This lake has a lot of opportunity in terms of larger fish that display different movements and behaviors than you may be used to on other lakes. Pass holds a lot of good surprises that way. Get used to looking for them, and your entire game there will change.

Dry-fly action can also be very good on the surface, but your opportunities are much more limited. You simply have to be there at the right time. Apart from a blatant, concentrated feed like the *Callibaetis* hatch, at times you'll spot fish out in the open, randomly cruising and rising. You may or may not identify a food source at that point. The most common time of day I've taken advantage of is late evening, when dusk turns to dark. The window is short, but the action can be good. I can't tell you in that circumstance whether, for example, a dry fly or streamer is the better choice. There's one way to find out. Beyond that, when I give chase via floater and dry fly, I do best by following the rises and sighting them up as much as possible. Again, look beyond the location of their heads and consider what they can see. The open areas at Pass can have a lot of water between feeding fish. If the action is on top, you may end up short of breath from moving around if you plan to connect a lot.

The depths can be more challenging than other areas at Pass, both in determining the presence of fish and in covering water effectively. It's more of a grind, but it can be done—and at times it's the place to be, like it or not. Again, by depths I mean 10 to 15 feet or so. Besides, Pass doesn't get much deeper than that.

With this game, a lot of anglers prefer to use a fish finder. I like the sport of finding them with a fly, and more often than not, it's a more reliable method than a screen with electronic data. I've run into plenty of anglers who "see fish" but can't figure out why they won't bite. Here's what I know: The fly won't lie. Go down with some confidence and be diligent. If fish are present and are to be taken, you'll connect; otherwise, who cares what a screen tells you. No sensor exists that can tell you how hungry fish are, or anything else that determines whether they'll strike. A simple two-dollar fly will do all that, if presented well.

Pass will reward trolling to an extent, but you have better options most of the time. I have the best success doing a cast-troll-strip-repeat presentation. On the troll, I'll give it a minute or so before stripping back each time, just long enough to get it down and tell me if a flat-out troll would be better. This way, you're considering the entire water column and can adjust to a certain depth if strikes are more prevalent there. On the whole, most of my strikes come on the strip. My theory is, fish simply react more to a faster, more aggressive retrieve. And remember, these trout have been afforded the opportunity to stay in the water, thrive, and grow with the benefit of catch-and-release.

As for location, I usually choose the outer shoals and immediately beyond as my first priority when searching deep. A good secondary stretch is anywhere just out from shore, because of the general contours of the lake bottom (this holds true for most lakes).

YOUR BUSY SCHEDULE

Now that we've laid out the basic elements of navigating Pass, the real key to the kingdom lies with timing. We touched on it earlier in the book, and it bears further mention in any discussion about Pass. Every outing of mine is spent making the best observations and decisions I can, and hopefully doing the right things. But at some point, I'll always be subject to those elements not in my control. I don't decide when, where, and how these fish are going to get active. I can only go and discover which cards will be dealt that day. So to take best advantage of the hand, I need to allow a full day, or as much of one as I am able. In this way I live by their schedule—my only option, since they really don't care what my schedule is.

Unfortunately, there is no substitute for hours spent on the water watching, waiting, and being available to respond. Something can be said for use of the information from recent outings, but you can only make an educated guess about when and where fish will show up. Still, a lot of the game is plain old being there at the ready. Again, I've seen countless times when the lake will empty out around dinner after a slow day, and as the last couple of anglers are still putting away at the launch, the action turns on like a light. The few who stuck around spend the remainder of the evening with bent rod in hand. Interestingly, our schedule is one of the more challenging things to control in this sport, yet that simple item probably determines more of your outcome in a day than anything else.

TIME MANAGEMENT

This is a little different than simply freeing up your schedule and planting yourself out there all day, but I place the priority equally as high. What I'm referring to here is how you manage your time once on the water. Over the years, I've discovered the direct benefits of constantly watching the clock throughout the entire day. When you measure every decision you make—and every method you try—in a time-bound manner, you become exponentially more efficient on the water. In the course of an outing, the results add up to a big number. I time everything I do, from tracking coverage of a certain area to measuring all the intervals between strikes. Then, throughout the day, I constantly use that information to tweak my approach and, hopefully, to stay on fish. Sounds rather mechanical and workmanlike, but I'm there to catch fish, and this is another discipline that cannot be ignored.

TROUT AND BAD BEHAVIOR

Fish Pass Lake long enough, and you'll observe certain habits or behaviors start to recur among its population. This is certainly not unique to Pass; every lake has its own "personality" in terms of often-repeated bad behavior. Here I'll identify the more recognizable ones, along with a helpful hint or two about dealing with them.

Short Strike. The least favorite among most anglers. Again, it's not you. These fish might be on one end or the other of a major feed, so your timing would be just slightly off. Enjoy the flurry of strikes, and adjust your expectations on landing to maybe 20 percent instead of the usual 80 percent. Pass is probably more famous for driving anglers up the wall with this due to the sheer size of its average inhabitant. The swats can come hard and furious, and if you don't let all the missing and losing get to you, it's rather fun. Here your best play is to take the beating and enjoy. Oh, and remember that half the time you're ahead of the feed, so stick around for the outcome. Either they straighten up and get serious about sticking, or the action stops. You may as well stay there and find out.

On Again, Off Again. A cousin of the short strike. These are usually prevalent at depth, and again, the strikes can nearly knock you out. Seems they're well hooked, but then—for no logical reason—about halfway in they just disappear from your hook. Like the short strike, it's not you. The takes are just awkward and ineffective, and I suspect the behavior roots from much the same situation as the short strike. Perhaps their deeper location makes for a different angle on the hook, and they stuck just a little better. Be aware that harder hook sets generally don't cure this one. Follow the same course of action as the short strike, and remember to have fun.

Slippery at Surface. Common with *Callibaetis* and other surface fare. Fly choice is your best cure at times. Grab that emerger mentioned earlier. Also remember the information about *Callibaetis* tactics. The timing and easy touch of that hook set solves the rest of the equation. The good news is, unlike the previous two circumstances, you can generally do something about this one.

Stubborn at Surface. They're feeding all around you, just not on your fly. This can be straight rises, or cruising and sipping—any form of visible feeding. Seems like a sure bet at first, until you get ignored by a hundred active trout. This one goes against my chosen tactic for stubborn minnow feeding near shore. This is a different situation, in that you don't necessarily have other, better-located fish as an option. Usually these are it. The food source is generally something small or unidentifiable, midges perhaps. Most times, your best play is simply sticking around and patiently waiting for a behavior change. Sounds counterintuitive, and I can't necessarily explain the behavior on this one. I just know from experimentation that, in a reasonable length of time, they usually get less finicky and more accepting of other options—like your fly. When they finally come around, I tend to take them underwater on the strip, anywhere from an inch below surface to several feet down. That leech of mine works; a smaller nymph (such as a Gold-Ribbed Hare's Ear) is also often a good choice when presenting up near the film.

Stubborn along Shoreline. That minnow feed is a good example, and I've also seen it with damsels: fish whipping along the shoreline, feeding to beat all, yet too busy and focused to be bothered by your measly offering. He's right there. He's crushing everything in sight on the surface. Time and time again, he obviously sees your fly, yet no amount of casting in the same spot will draw him, or chase him out. He just keeps going about his business—and business is good without you! If neither dry nor streamer/nymph works, his obvious play is to not only beat you himself, but also to beat you for all his buddies by occupying as much of your time as possible. Another good reason to join my "watch the clock" program. By now you know the cure: just walk away from him and go chase his buddies out from shore. Recall the logic here. You need to tip the odds your way by finding other fish, in a larger, less-visible area, with less food competition. Usually it isn't far away.

The Lone Riser. Be warned before you give chase via float tube. He casually meanders along, rising in rhythm at a pace just faster than you can move to keep up. What a coincidence. And if his path continues in a straight line, he's not stopping for you. I'll give chase for a short duration if there are directional changes that favor me, and if I can actually keep up. Otherwise don't bother chasing him into parts unknown at the other end of the lake without oars. The simple fact that he was there on the feed may serve you—tipping you off to other catchable fish nearby, perhaps just not visible. When giving chase has not been an option, I've had success with the "pie-cutting" drill (see page 113).

BROWN TROUT AT PASS

If Pass had nothing else, her browns would be enough to keep me happy. Since we exhausted the subject in another lesson, I'll keep it short and relate a few things to Pass. Although the sample we looked at came from different locations, the conclusions drawn certainly apply here. And take the five-to-one (rainbows-to-browns) rule with a big grain of salt. Over the course of the year it generally irons out, but on any given day, the ratio can be anything. My advice is, don't just wait for them to come into shore to give chase. True, they're famous for that at Pass, but it only accounts for a fraction of the opportunity. All the other areas we've talked about will hold them at different times, and in all sizes. Yes, they prefer low lighting, but don't hold yourself to that, either. As with other trout, the rules are all meant to be broken. Older browns don't just stick to heavy cover and dark shadows to lay in wait for ambush. Put enough on the menu and they'll come out all hours, in any section of water, to chase it down. Look for the following common signs and opportunities at Pass:

Those Fins and Tails. They can be spotted anywhere, but again, the shoreline is famous for this feeding ritual near surface. Take a really cautious approach, keeping in mind they are very visible that close to the surface—and they know it. Use a small presentation, work their field of vision, and don't even think of slapping their dorsal with your cast. If you can't draw the take, congratulations: You're normal.

The Dog Splash. I'm always dying to know what's going on here. I'd hate to be the subject of that attack. At best these usually tell you that active browns are feeding in the area: big ones. Obviously stick around and get to work. That fast retrieve that I like can be well received here.

The Boiler. Look for him against shore during spring. It doesn't happen all the time, but when it does, you may see the behavior for several outings. Again, it's all about the food source. You'll see a small surface disturbance that literally looks like a little circle of boiling water. The cause is feeding from just below the surface; the food is sipped in while the fish slowly circles the area. A full surface break never happens. Likely these larger fish are conserving energy and are wary of visibility, given the position of their bodies. A less-experienced eye will pass the sign off as a smaller fish unworthy of the chase, but in nearly every case, the behavior is the clear mark of a mature brown. The fun here is all in the approach: you'll want to go in with a very small and subtle presentation. Grab that Pablo's Cripple. Takes are generally understated, and you won't realize what you have for a time. Often they won't even react to your hook set at first. You'll know when he's truly onto you when he takes an immediate turn south and runs to the bottom. Game on and pray no structure sits underneath you. Beyond that, enjoy the gift you've been given and don't be in a hurry. He'll come up when he feels like it.

When You See Just One. Whether by sight or by hookup, keep in mind that a single brown begets another, and another. They're famous for coming out *en masse*, and since we don't see them often enough, always work to turn one into many.

Dusk. The ideal low-lighting situation. They make a hobby out of subduing themselves in cover, where they can look out and have just enough light to see their next meal swim by. Now is the time to grab a section of shoreline and pick it apart.

Spring and Fall. Take advantage of those ideal water temperatures. Browns will be active at all hours and can be found in any location. Check the banks often, but don't live there all day if you're not seeing action. In these seasonal conditions, browns will be anything but bashful along shore, so you shouldn't have any problem detecting them.

Shoreline Facts and Myths
- The only good place to search for browns: Myth.
- The only good place to search for large browns: Myth.
- It's a good idea to keep at it if nothing is showing, so hold out for that single brown over a three-hour period: Myth.

Pass Lake browns are taken regularly near dusk when the lighting starts to dim. Leeches, minnows and other similar patterns are highly effective.

- Smart to search the shoreline often in periods of low light, visible food, or ideal temperatures: Fact.
- One brown against the bank is a very good indicator of more: Fact.
- Big white streamers, or go home—no matter what: Myth.
- They hang out there all night, every night: Myth.
- You get one strike and that's it: Myth.
- Once hooked, if it comes off it's gone. I'd say Fact for the most part; however, on occasion I've hooked the same fish a second time on a dry fly when the first hookup lasted a short time.

Night Fishing. When burning the late-night oil at Pass, remember all the safety rules: phone, a partner, good lighting, avoiding extreme cold, etc. At times, fishing alone may be your only option. In those cases, take good precautions at the very least, and only head out alone if you're already very familiar with the terrain. I'm not the most experienced night angler, but I do know the darkness does not necessarily equal good fishing. Many times the bite happens at dusk, only to go quiet when the bats come out.

When the action is on, the open surface can be a lot of fun because of all that limited visibility. Any method can work at one time or another, but I usually prefer to strip underwater using something with a little size. I imagine most anglers would prefer a floater here, and I won't argue. For me, a sinker is what I'm more used to. The shoreline can also be a lot of fun, and I find it's possible to adjust to the dark and avoid hanging it up reasonably well. A couple of times hanging up is usually motivation enough to figure it out. And if hanging it up is a real weakness, give the roadside stretches a try. Those headlights can provide good visibility if the cars don't drive you nuts. Moreover, those stretches of shoreline are generally worth patrolling.

Playing and Landing. The way you play them at Pass once hooked really is a game changer. Given the lake population's average size and the energy they display most of the year, a few of the right habits will still yield you a consistently high percentage to the net. Short of those behavioral issues we talked about, you can expect around 80 percent every time out.

Assuming your hook is sharp, make it your life goal to never—ever—allow even an inch of slack from hook set to landing. This is the number-one mistake out there by a long shot, and those fish will know what to do with it. I won't rehash my argument for avoiding use of the reel here, but give this some serious thought. For me, it has a lot to do with that 80-percent success rate, and I have yet to see anyone go back to the old way after being introduced to this method. Beyond that, keeping the fight close, even underneath you, gives you the nod on control. I also keep the rod lower to the water with fish in so close; and if a good run takes the tip under, that's even better. Finally, you don't want them completely tired out, but be just patient enough to bring them up without a major fuss at the surface. It should be a nice smooth track to the net, with head slightly lifted. If anything, err on the side of big in terms of size for your net. Mine has a 17-inch bow, and I wouldn't go much smaller at Pass.

Fishing Reports. Highly encouraged and, if anything, I'd love to see more anglers sharing them. As a reader, here's what you need to know: Most reports about Pass are only useful if you make them that way. That is, you'll want a good filter system as you read, realizing both that the success stories largely apply to one particular day, and also that those reports of slow fishing almost never describe the whole picture out there. The next time you read a report, consider everything discussed here and think of all the possible reasons why an angler might have missed out. (The list is endless.) Remember, those reports are just as useful as the successful ones. If an experienced fly fisher went out from seven o'clock in the morning until noon, worked the far end diligently, had the same clear weather as what's forecast for my outing, and says there was zero action—that gives me a good head start. It still may or may not mean mornings are worth showing up, but at least I now have a piece of the puzzle. Point is, with Pass I'd never write the place off. Virtually any day, short of icing over, the lake will produce plenty for anyone able to solve the puzzle.

Angling Pressure. If your impression of the lake is one of crowds and "walking across the boats," as they say, give it a try outside of early spring. I say this all the time, but Pass will produce at any time of year, and most career days take place outside of early spring. Again, it's entirely a function of conditions and circumstances, and to that end, anything can happen at any time.

Reality Check. It doesn't take rocket science to wear your net out at Pass. Solving the puzzle—or catching more fish—is the simple result of a combination of little things. Most factors may be subtle, but they add up. Given its favorable regulations, along with a good handful of other advantages, Pass will afford unusually lopsided results to anyone willing to work for them. The lake may seem no better than any other at first, providing a nice fish or two for a day's effort. Be aware that a lot lives down there, just waiting for you to figure things out. And the best thing I can say about preconceived expectations is you're smart to avoid them. At Pass they can easily disappoint or, worse, serve as a limitation. I almost never find a report that matches my own experiences out there. Again, reports may provide a start, but I wouldn't lean on them beyond that. Your best move in every case is to lean on your own box of tools. Depending on a lot of factors, including your experience, a good take at Pass can be anything from 7 to 70—or beyond. So enjoy the hand you're dealt in a day, and make the best of it. Finally, Pass Lake is a good venue for building a lot of skills that transfer to other lakes and ponds. Many of Pass's personality traits won't repeat elsewhere, but I can't name a better place locally to develop your ability to solve puzzles.

Miscellany. The lake is generally well cared for, however I still make it a habit to pick up where the need arises. I would encourage anyone who wets a line there to carry extra plastic and pitch in often. A place in our back yard that fishes this well deserves the extra care, so I treat it like my own property. And to that end, I'm not averse to contributing a little enforcement when necessary. It's not often, but every year Pass gets its share of those unaware of the rules (or claiming to be). You and I are in the best position to cure that, and we're also the beneficiaries of it. I would say, to the extent that it's safe, it's our privilege to help out with enforcement. I don't mean strong-arming here, just polite, respectful confrontation and nothing further. In my experience, that's all it ever takes. Lastly, the local club usually provides catch record cards at the launch. Look for them at the sign by the picnic table. The information you provide is voluntary but helps them tremendously in their efforts to manage the fishery. It's a good ritual every time you take out.

Obviously this is only one lake, and no two of them are alike. The level of detail provided here may be very specific to a single location in the Pacific Northwest, but you should now have a pretty good picture of how to pick apart any lake and develop the same kind of familiarity. Again, the time invested will show well in your results, and better still, you'll learn a surprising amount of new things about stillwater fly fishing during the process. And that knowledge will serve you anywhere you go.

Lesson 5

ANATOMY OF AN OUTING

In this lesson, I'll pick apart an actual outing to illustrate some of the material we've shared so far. A note about numbers: Earlier in the book I mentioned the importance of knowing when to stop in terms of your catch rate and its potential impact on the fish. In the following scenarios, I'm using fish count as a tangible and relatable means to measure results. Keep in mind that 5 fish to me probably means something different than 5 fish to you, or to someone else. However, I think there is good value in reporting to you whether an approach produced 5 fish, 50 fish, or something in between. But by no means am I encouraging undue pressure on any lake environment. Always raise the question of impact when having success with rod and reel. For this exercise, we'll navigate the same body of water as Lesson 4. Now that you're familiar with Pass Lake, we can go a step further by spending a virtual day there with rod and reel. I also chose timing and conditions that fall in the middle in terms of how active the lake is. This gives us a nice balance of hardship and results, therefore describing the majority of days we spend on the water.

With that in mind, I'm hoping what follows is found to be meaningful and useful.

PREFUNCTIONING

Here's what I know before arriving: The lake had been in the same feeding pattern for weeks before the first of our fall storms recently blew in. Surface temperatures finally dropped to below 60 degrees F for the first time in months, and with the change to more fall-like conditions, I'm expecting the predominant evening feed to start spreading out through the day. For the most part, the younger plants have owned daytime for a while, giving way to older generations, 15 inches and above, later in the evenings. The food source for these larger fish has been minnows, by the bucketful, that show mostly in later hours toward dark. Makes sense, as these fish have every reason to lay low in the warmer and brighter part of the day. They may as well stay hidden until the desirable combination of more calories and less visibility occurs toward day's end. Now that it's almost November, I'm pretty sure I'll see a good mix of planters, along with their older cousins, throughout most of this outing. In terms of numbers, peak time in November will usually yield a catch of 40 or so for an entire day.

This trip marks the first weekend of typical fall weather, so I'm thinking the better action is just getting started and should continue to accelerate throughout the month. It does that every year, short of a freak weather occurrence. Today the weather will start out clear and cool and then give way to a system of clouds and wind by late morning. Add it all up, and 30 fish is probably a good target for today. This year, about half those should be the smaller planters. Most of the time this lake puts out larger fish, but occasionally these new plants mix in. At the moment, the lake isn't showing many fish in the mid-teen range. Instead, a gap exists between the smaller 11-inch ones and the larger 16- to 18-inch ones—which are now on a whole separate feeding pattern, given their dietary needs at that size. In my experience, the smaller fish will hold the same feeding habits until they hit about 15 inches, and then their behavior takes a turn in search of higher caloric intake. So, when the lake is at its best, a good generation of 14-inch trout swims along with the next generation up—typically 18–plus inches— which haven't hit the first stages of major attrition as yet. Last fall was like that. This year's cards are different, so I'll take the hand I'm dealt and be content with it.

GAME TIME

At 7:15 a.m., I pull up roadside and it's almost as quiet as it is dark. First light is minutes away, so I hustle into my waders and get ready to put in. Closing in on 7:30, the lake looks rather peaceful and uninhabited. I snap a shot or two of the lake and early sky and then get at it. Once out, I can see a couple of anglers getting in at the launch. With any luck, we'll share some recon later today. So far no signs of food or fish, and it looks like 54 degrees F is our surface temp. I can definitely live with that, as mid-50s should have them active all day. A good section of shoreline cover leads from my put-in to the bay, and I decide that's a good place to start. I've hit fish along this section recently, so I'm curious to see if anything holds there this morning. Down to the drain pipe and not one strike, so I back out toward the middle of the bay and start working the open water.

As usual, I'm starting the day with the leech I had on from last time. I take a good sampling of the bay, both near surface and at depth, and still not a single strike. Time check: 13 minutes is a good enough sample of the area, so I'm off to troll toward the first shoal, about 4 minutes away. Nothing hits as I move across, even after a couple of retrieves. Within maybe 60 yards of shore, I know I'm moving over the edge of the outer shoal. I stop and begin working the open area. Nothing after a few casts, and as I work, I'm looking in every direction for anything that may resemble a clue.

I see my first rise closer to shore. He's not in tight, but at least something is active midway along the shoal. I move to within 40 yards or so and begin throwing toward the outer part of the shallow hedges. Second cast and first fish on, pretty good rainbow. Another time check after the release, and I've been in just over 20 minutes. The next fish comes within a few more casts, and then I move around, working that same area. I also check both sides of the shoal to see if the action extends very far outward. It appears everything is pretty central along mid-shoal. I land another five there (plus one lost) before the sun finally comes over the trees and hits the water. I give it a few more minutes just to see if it livens up from the light, but, as I suspect, it dies off. Now it's after nine o'clock. I decide to stay out of the sun and head back across toward the bay, where the entire shoreline will remain in the shade for the next few hours. As I move across, I observe the other two anglers have decided to work the opposite shoreline. The sun is directly on it, but I'll continue to watch and see if they're having luck over there.

The bay now has a small midge hatch coming off, pretty light, but I decide to spend a few minutes and see if any feeders are on it. I work toward the shaded area, and it seems little or nothing is going on. Finally a planter comes up, and I continue working that area in search of more. A few minutes later, I decide that this hatch is good for an occasional planter if enough work goes in. Not worth it.

By now I'm next to the weedy section, where the shoreline separates from the road for the last time. Not expecting much, I make my way down, moving from right to left. After a dozen casts, I decide to give it one or two more before putting it deep and commuting to the other end of the lake. Next cast, first brown on—chases it out, misses it, and comes back on it

These two came on consecutive casts against shore. When signs are that good, you're smart to hold still and work the immediate section thoroughly. Making another pass within a few minutes is also recommended.

just in front of me. I'll gladly take this 15-incher. Then two more rainbows right after (plus another loss). As I continue along, the action stops; I know I'm past the zone. I decide to turn around and come back through a few minutes later.

Usually when you see that many fish in a small section of shoreline, it's a good bet to wait a short time and go back through. I'm giving myself a 50/50 chance of picking up one more strike in that little zone. This time it doesn't pay off, so I move farther down and work the shoreline near the long parallel log after the curve. A little farther down, I pick up one more planter and figure it's time to make the commute to the other end. While trolling, I scribble some notes and grab a quick snack. At the same time, I realize that I haven't noticed any action from the anglers across the way, and they look like pretty good fly fishers. So far, I'm probably in the right place.

After those midges in the bay, there probably won't be much, if anything, in terms of visible food. So from now on, I'm likely in for a day of blind searching. I know the minnows will come out strong this evening, but until then, I think I'm on my own. Then again, with 54-degree water, I'm not too upset. In these conditions, fish will be out in search of food all day. I don't need an abundance of clues, as long as I can cover water, follow strikes, and manage time effectively.

Looking toward the other end of the lake, I notice an eagle working the corner section pretty hard. Who knows, it may mean something. He doesn't stick around long, but I'll tuck that away. I can work the weeds on my way down and get there in the next 10 minutes or so. Where the weeds begin, I start casting toward shore again. The action is OK; another planter comes up, along with a nicer rainbow. Then I see a good one roll right against the weeds. I slow down and take a breath, set up, and lay it in perfectly. The grab is instant, high enough that the surface pops on the take. Perfect hook set, but I manage to miss, and he's off. That hurts.

Next one is a better hook set, but he decides not to stick around for long either. I'm calling the first one a missed strike, but the second is an outright lost fish. By this time I'm at the corner where the eagle had been. It's an easy section of shoal to cover and can be loaded with feeding fish at the right time. Unfortunately, this is not one of those times. I miss one smaller fish in a few minutes' time and, after enough of a sample, it's time to move on.

The other end of the lake is basically an extended shoal that runs its entire width. It can be really productive in the open water—again, at the right time. I take two planters in a few minutes and decide to work the shoreline across the back while it's still in the shade. Another nice one comes up, and that's all I'm getting. I hit the open again. By now it's going on eleven o'clock, and the clouds promised in the weather report start rolling in, along with some wind. I'm hoping this is good news, since visibility should cut way down if the sky darkens and the surface starts showing good chop.

I start working the open shoal, both shallow and at depth, and at first nothing comes calling. Eventually a few planters come around, and it seems that's about all there is at this part of the day. I'll take them for now. As early afternoon takes over, the weather is a mixed bag of off-and-on clouds and wind, so the sunlight isn't going to go away for good. I had hoped for an outright turn to overcast skies, surface chop, and maybe some rain—but it's not in the cards today. That sunlight will continue to cramp my style, so the action ends up grinding along through midafternoon: fishable, but no feeding frenzy. Besides that, the two anglers from earlier have since turned back, so no running into them or sharing any recon. Bummer.

Next I hit the weedy shoreline from the middle corner to the point that borders the right side of the bay. Only one more planter is there, so I hit the big open area toward the rock face to the west. This is another productive area at times, and a favorite among the Chironomid set, but again, not today. More blind searching before I move in toward another good section of weedy shoreline. By now, the wind is hitting that part of the bank head-on, so visibility is really restricted in the shallows. I've done well in this situation before. This time it works out, as several fish, including my second brown, come out before it goes quiet. From there, I hit some of the water just out from the bank then continue leftward along shore. It's a treed section with great cover, but it provides no action at the moment.

By now it's going on two o'clock, and, though it's been a grind, at 28, I'm looking better than expected for this time of day. Sure, half of those are planters, but I'll gladly take the number of nice ones so far. The bite is also slowing down pretty hard, and I'm starving, so this is a good time to get out and have lunch. I'm not in a hurry at this point, since I figure there won't be much action till it gets closer to evening.

You can get pretty good at predicting numbers for a day, given a particular set of factors. Fluctuation in activity can also be predicted as the day wears on. In this case, I'm ahead of plan right now, so I know things will balance out in the form of slower action for the remainder of the day. I've

A shallow weedy shoreline can be highly productive at times. Note the surface chop; often this is all it takes to bring them in.

seen that go both ways many times. When action comes on early, I know to get all I can, and, conversely, when it's slow early, I'm ready to make it up in a late rally. It's amazing how consistent that is, and it lends great support to the idea that they have to come out and feed some time. It's just a matter of when, and of your being there when it happens.

As I sit and enjoy a sandwich, I can see a few other anglers have shown up; a couple of them are making their way across the far end. I can't tell how they're doing from this distance, but I can see they're working together, one along the shoreline, the other in the open. Great way to cover water when paired up. Before finishing up, I plan out the afternoon, deciding to stay put in this area for maybe 30 minutes before working my way up the shoreline toward the first shoal. My logic is, I'll get one more good sample of the immediate area and, unless I hit the jackpot, work the north shoreline once in full shade.

After lunch I get back in and start working a rocky section along the bank, before heading back toward the bay. The shoreline gives up a nice one, and then I notice one of the two anglers from earlier is headed my way along shore. Still at a distance, I could reverse my direction and go up the shoreline early, well ahead of him. I decide that, if I were him, it would be a lot nicer to fish virgin shoreline back to the near-side of the lake.

Change of plan: I'll pull away from the bank and go work the open section of the outer bay while he moves through. I notice he's using a floater, so I'm also curious about the section he just worked. It lit up pretty well a little earlier for me, so I decide to try it again with my sinker before committing to the open water. Zip. I don't think he's missing anything; those fish have just moved out. But sure enough, the open water is void as well, so I work a short time and give the other angler a chance to advance up shore. Maybe 15 minutes behind him, I start moving up, shoreline now fully shaded. Nothing early on, so maybe pulling out and trolling back is a better move. If there's no action here, I may as well hit the next destination that much sooner and make better use of the time.

No luck during the commute either, and by now I've had only one in the last two hours, lunch notwithstanding. I start wondering how well the late afternoon and early evening will hold up, since more fish were active early in the day.

Nearing the first shoal from this morning, I see a nice section of cover along shore that often holds fish. Change of plan again: It just *looks* fishy, and I can work through without taking long. Two good ones come out and then a planter in the open just out from the right edge of the shoal. Hopefully that's a good sign, and I'll start getting into them. By now it's late afternoon and the area is well occupied—five anglers, including me. If the outer edge will produce, I'm fine to stick around. But none of us is really hooking up. Yet another change of plan: I do a 180-degree turn and go back to the area right of the shoal where I had taken those three. I get one more, a pretty good brown, but I'm spending too much time without enough action.

Now I look across toward the bay and contemplate it as an alternative, since the main shoal is full of anglers and void of fish. A little more thought, and I decide it's a timing thing. The sun is about to fall, and I can see minnows are beginning to pop tight to shore around the shoal. Besides, in the past, I've gone across only to hit one or two in prime time, when probably several more could've been had over here, where most of the food is. That's not always the case, but at the moment, these minnows are clearly centered around the shoal where all this heavy vegetation is. Decision made, and I wait out the sunset in hopes of something good.

About an hour before dark, it finally picks up. No frenzy, but the shoal, now void of anglers at this late hour, gives up another five before lights out. And sure enough, those fish rolling on minnows in the shallow weeds prove not to be the best prospect. This food source is in its latter stages, and the combination of high visibility in the shallows and a bazillion minnows means a single offering creates a deceptively poor prospect with a fly rod. I made only enough casts to confirm that and then spent the other 95 percent of my time on the outer shoal, resisting temptation. Those last five were the payoff, and I gladly took them.

When the remaining daylight disappears, so does the action. All told, 10 hours yielded 37 to the net and another 3 lost today, with those planters making up about half. Only 3 brownies, but all were good-sized, and that beats going without. The action came in spurts, with most centered around midday and late afternoon into evening.

Looking back, it's been a pretty good outing overall. Sure enough, fall action is just getting started, and I didn't find this day to be too unusual. Plenty of small surprises throughout the day, but I think the WHEN–WHERE–HOW–WHAT method did its job, as did having an open mind and some willingness to improvise. Though there were not many, there were enough clues to reasonably solve the puzzle. For me, it was a combination of general knowledge about the lake, a little recon from last weekend, observation of food (though limited), watching other anglers, and some interpretation of current conditions. And still, it took quite a bit of blind searching and time management throughout the day. Oh, and that leech of mine was there from first to final cast, so I can't say fly selection was ever part of the equation.

In this case, I think the time management part was responsible for a lot of the success. The more I fish stillwater, the more I look at my watch and measure everything by it. I realize this goes against the idea of getting away and losing track of the time, but then again, I'm not about to ditch something that effective just because it doesn't fit some imaginary ideal scenario.

Lesson 6

SOLUTIONS FOR SLOW DAYS

There is something of value to understand about slow conditions. Although anything can happen, it's much more rare than common to have inactivity last an entire day. And once you have a working knowledge of WHEN and WHERE to locate holding or feeding trout, you may find you seldom or almost never encounter extended inactivity—or at least encounter it less frequently. That's all fine and good, but what about those dead days, since they can still rear their heads occasionally? At times you can do everything right, and it's still unavoidable. However, you do have some ability to control whether it's a dead day by the time you leave. Usually *dead* means slow, which is different from altogether stopped. And we can still do something about slow, however limited our control may be.

Here, it comes down to your own subjective priorities and perception of rewards, since many don't feel their time is well spent in really slow or dead conditions. For me, I've worked through an endless number of them and have learned how to produce fish when there are seemingly none to be had. You can't call a day dead if you can make something out of it. In my experience, a combination of confidence, patience, staying out there, and doing the stuff we've been talking about will turn nearly any dead day into a respectable outing.

Here is my thought process when things are slow: For one, they can't hide all day without feeding, and often it's a matter of confidently waiting them out. The solution to the puzzle, even when difficult, nearly always shows itself by day's end. If nothing else, decide that the feed has to happen by dark, and look for a good push as dusk approaches. On most slow or dead days, this invariably happens. Often I'll see nearly every angler on the lake take out and go home just before it gets good. I've watched a lot of

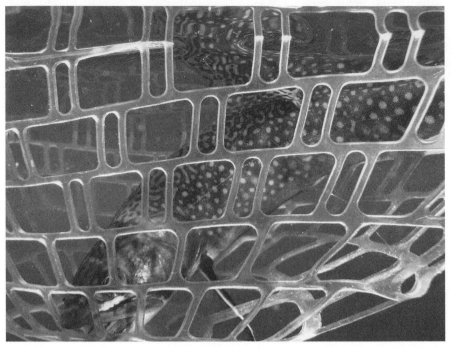

Many who define a reward only by number or size will find little or none during slow periods. Tough lessons and hard-earned fish are certainly worthwhile in their own right, and sometimes a handsome catch like this mountain brookie is reward enough.

anglers still loading up boats and putting stuff away at the launch as the first good bite of the day turns on like a light, and those of us left spend the entire last hour or two with rod bent.

Also consider that, at certain times, the most ideal feeding conditions may occur overnight—when all good anglers are safe in their beds. That doesn't mean the lake will be entirely void of activity during daylight hours, but it may explain times when a population of trout seems to be on a diet. Lastly, remember this about dead conditions: at first you might not be able to tell if it's truly slow or dead, or if it's just you. That's OK. Once you spend some time at it, you'll have the experience and confidence to know for sure—or at least make the best educated guess as to why activity acts as it does.

In the Pacific Northwest, where I live, the mild climate allows stillwater fly fishers to pursue their craft as a year-round endeavor. In so doing, we regularly find ourselves in conditions in which our cup does not exactly runneth over with good viable clues. If only the water would stay 55 degrees all year, and abundant food sources would show up every time out.

The unfortunate reality is that damsels have their day, just as midges, mayflies, and minnows have theirs, when nature suits it. The rest of the time they disappear, leaving us with little more than faith to go on. Does it mean we should stop fishing when the clues go away? No, not a chance. Lack of clues and slow activity only make for a better puzzle. This is what you look for after solving so many easy puzzles that they have become less interesting. It means you love to fish as much as ever, but you need a better challenge, and you finally want to get good at it. *Good* means being able to solve the puzzle in the absence of easy clues, regularly turning a skunking into a respectable outing. We get good at our sport from showing up and working through those clueless days. Good will also mean going back when the clues are there, seeing them in a new way, and obliterating good opportunities every time they present themselves. More on that later.

By now you're probably realizing these changes in thought and method will alter the way you spend time on the water. Right now, you may really enjoy spending the day in a mindless state of peaceful bliss out there. I get that, and I relate to that. I still spend some of my days doing the same exact thing. Rest assured, you're not going to have to give up the experience you've always treasured. Rather, you're now going to be able to address all that mystery and overcome the parts of angling that have left you in a frustrated quandary your entire life as a stillwater fly fisher. In the end, you'll be equipped to solve the puzzle when you wish—and when you'd prefer the old, relaxing experience, it'll still be there waiting for you, as always. Control is a very good thing, and after this you'll have much more of it.

Let's establish what a slow day should look like—not so much in terms of conditions, but in terms of your results. Perhaps the lake had been doing just fine prior to now, but the time of year has brought on the slow action, or maybe a sudden weather change has put the fish temporarily down. Whatever the reason, you're in for a day of little or no visible clues: not much food in the water, no fish showing at surface, and strikes anything but abundant. Maybe they're even nonexistent at first.

One more thing: On a slow day, a number of other anglers will accompany you on the water throughout the day; however, each of them will end with zero to two fish. Maybe one guy gets four or five for his efforts. Yet in the face of all that, by reading the clues, you manage to exploit a few obscure opportunities—possibly just one or two—but you were still able to turn each into a good number of fish landed. By the time you take out you've landed 14, or maybe you ended up gunning for 20 and just missed, or maybe you gunned for 20 and actually hit 26 because that section of shoreline lit up like a Christmas tree at midday. Good thing you found it and knew what to do with it. And if you made that happen, chances are you were the one person at the lake that day who cracked the code, reasonably solved the puzzle, and finished with a surprisingly good outing despite so few clues and so little activity. Most days, on most lakes, it never happens, regardless of how many show up. But if having that kind of success time after time is how you'd like to fish, by all means read on.

In this lesson, we'll take some of the concepts previously learned, along with some new ones, and apply them to an outing short on clues and activity. No surprise, the first tool you'll need—to go from a near skunking to an unusually good solution to the puzzle—is confidence. On any day of the year, regardless of circumstances, always start with this. Your confidence directly affects everything you do on the water, and it will matter more than ever on these slower days. Being confident in your experience and abilities, along with the belief that there really is no bad outcome, will give you the best mindset for success. You have the opportunity to learn every time out, regardless of results, and anytime you learn, you get better. That means a slow outing, even a skunking, has value. And it's your job as a good fly fisher to make it pay, in terms of what you walk away with. Think of every outing the same way, and those days of zero to two will disappear on their own.

Now that the pressure is off, let's turn faith into fish.

For starters, not all lakes are equal when it comes to the off-season or slow parts of the year. Much of that occurs in winter, when several months may go by with cooler water temperatures in some regions and lakes frozen altogether in others. Ice notwithstanding, certain lakes will fish better during this time because of any combination of factors, including stocks, pressure throughout the year, regulations, depth, terrain, elevation, and more. Your first order of business will be to find a small handful of the most relevant factors and target them when all the clues disappear. Along those lines, some of the better spring and summer lakes may be lousy prospects when temperatures fall. And to complicate matters, it's not always the same list of lakes that produce best in slow conditions, although some are more consistent than others. Finding your own list is not as difficult as it may sound, and once you have it, you're usually set. Lastly, I'm generally referring to lowland lakes in winter, simply because they go hand in hand with slow action and few clues; however, the lesson would apply to any lake at any time, since slow action can rear its head whenever and wherever it wants.

Opportunity. The good news is, you'll use a very simple strategy in slower conditions. Overall, you're looking for the limited number of opportunities that occur in a day, and then exploiting the most out of each. Some days you'll be lucky to find even one or two of these opportunities, so without exception, the exploiting part is an absolute must. Think of your entire day in terms of only two activities: You're either looking for an opportunity or taking advantage of one. An opportunity is the chance to turn a strike into several or even many. As such, you'll want to view each strike as an opportunity to earn subsequent strikes. In going about it this way, you're operating on the principle that what one fish is doing, many are doing. And I'm a big believer in collective behavior among trout, because that assumption pays off in ways much too significant to ignore. So with any strike, you should assume that all the information associated with the strike is being relevant to other fish. That includes time of day, location, depth, food, type of behavior, and so on. At all times, slow and active days alike, try to continuously connect the dots from one fish to the next by way of this copycat principle.

TIME AND LOCATION

The Two-Dimensional Window. While searching, I always look for the window in terms of two dimensions, time and location. Let's look at how they relate to one another. Over the course of an outing, there may be one or more periods of time where the fish become active (the bite picks up). During this active part of the day, you work hard to hit all you can before it slows back down. Nothing complicated there. Now, throughout the day, as you move about the lake, you may also discover certain locations—maybe the shoals or perhaps over structure—where fish are holding. Just as you would with time, you take full advantage of these locations where you've found fish in numbers.

Once again, you pick the area over as effectively as you can to maximize your results before it dries up. There are specific ways of doing that, but for now we'll keep it simple. The point is, you have two viable dimensions with which to conduct a search, so you'll always want to consider both when on the water. Otherwise you're only conducting half the search available to you. I call that a severe handicap, and that's exactly what it is.

The other point is that these two dimensions are not mutually exclusive, meaning they overlap. So as you look for the open windows throughout the day, always seek the active time-spans and then the best locations within those time-spans. You need both. Right time, wrong location, is no better than right location, wrong time. This two-dimensional window is just another play on our WHEN and WHERE principle, only now we've drilled down to a basic search method for tough water. In short, even in slow conditions with little or no clues, trout will still gather and become active at the right time and location in a day. A good stillwater angler has the faith and confidence to believe it outright, and the ability to put himself into the heart of this two-dimensional window as many times as his dealt hand will afford. While often it may only be once, that's still more than enough, and a single opportunity, fully exploited, can pay handsomely.

Ticking Away the Moments. On slower days, the real key to your success will be to solve the puzzle in terms of time. You need both that and location, but time still comes as the first priority, and time will always matter more than place (WHEN comes before WHERE). Assuming you have most or all of the day to spend, as you work to zero in on the active part of it, you'll also want to manage the clock effectively. We covered this earlier as a suggested game changer, but now I'll revisit the idea with a bit more emphasis.

And if we're now viewing it on an advanced level, I'd say watching and using the clock is no longer a mere suggestion. This one becomes another requirement if you want to convert ho-hum results into something surprising on an otherwise dismal outing. I say that because it's the only way I know to make it happen.

Making effective use of your watch is really simple to execute. Any effort will come in the form of establishing a new habit. But like any good habit, once you have it, you have it for good. I use my watch throughout the day to measure everything from time spent on each method to intervals between strikes. That watch is my gauge, or speedometer, so I always know if I'm on track, or when to change up. In general I won't go more than 20 or 30 minutes before changing up if I'm not producing. Changing up can mean location, depth, method, or some combination of things.

And as you can guess, I wouldn't consider a different fly as a legitimate form of change up. In lakes, this is seldom or never the key ingredient. As you manage time, be sure and measure the things that matter. You're trying to put yourself where fish are located, not select the magic fly that draws them like a magnet from all directions. Trust me. If it worked like that, I'd be the first one doing it.

It's likely that when you start tracking time, you'll be surprised at how often you linger too long in any single location, or stick with any one method. If you think something "should" work, it just comes naturally to stay at it indefinitely. And unless you have a gauge that holds your behavior to logic instead of wishful thinking, you'll continue to waste your most valuable resource. I find it's impossible to track or manage time well without using a watch out there, and not doing so comes at a hefty price. In other words, when a day ends with zero or very few fish, lack of time management will be among the largest contributing factors. It's one of the most critical resources we have out there, and generally those who manage it end up worlds apart from those who don't.

The Value of a Good Trend. Another key concept introduced earlier. When conditions are slow or lacking in clues, you can bump your odds significantly with repeated trips to the same place. An angler who shows up armed with recent recon will already have a plan and a clear direction starting out. At more productive parts of the year—spring perhaps—trend information is certainly an advantage, but not as much a necessity to solve the day's puzzle as it is during slower times. When the clues readily present themselves over the course of a day, as with midges, you're getting most of the information handed to you just for being observant. But in mid-January, your hand of cards won't be so easy to play. In 40-degree F water, with no signs of food or movement, knowing WHEN and WHERE they were active yesterday or last week is a very welcome and useful tool to carry.

And again, last week's activity won't repeat exactly today—or ever. But a good percentage of it will probably still hold true, and that will provide you with the solution to a good part of today's puzzle. On slow days, this will usually determine the outing you have more than anything else. Just as with time management, arming yourself with trend information will separate you from those without by a long shot.

One other tip: Someone else's report can be helpful and useful, but it will never come close to replacing the information you gather on your own. And it doesn't matter how experienced the other angler is compared to you. No two of us fish alike, or have the same set of skills and abilities. Your own observations and methods for burying the hook will always be most useful to you when it comes to using the information next time. We all interpret and react differently to the events in a day, and making good on another guy's recon is rarely as easy as it sounds. Point is, there is no substitute for going out regularly and staying on top of the action. It's the only way I know to have consistent success in slower conditions. Obviously, you won't always have this information when the water suddenly goes cold or slow, but when the option is there, you'll want to take advantage.

OTHER TIMING STRATEGIES

Wait Them Out. We touched on this previously, only now it becomes a more significant part of your strategy. Often this is the only thing I have to go on in dead conditions. When on the water, if you're confident you are covering the place effectively and are still unable to find the action, always fall back on this principle. You can't control the timing of the bite, and you won't always know the recent trends where you fish. If the first half of your outing bears little or no fruit in the face of a good search effort, you can be confident that it's a simple matter of timing. Best thing you can do is just stay there and gear toward the rally. Some of the most fulfilling outings I've had in slow conditions were when I've put this one to use and made it pay. I get a lot of satisfaction from taking out at day's end knowing I solved the puzzle by remaining patient and confident.

And once rally time arrived and they got active, that overwhelming sensation of losing the game disappeared in a hurry. We also discussed this previously, but it's worth revisiting in a setting of slow conditions, since the day has a tendency to balance out in terms of feeding activity. In that way, if I do surprisingly well early on, I can count on the activity to taper off later in the day, and vice versa. This may not be the case at busier times of the year. However, when food is less prevalent and temperatures are not ideal, this balancing effect nearly always occurs out there.

Once you dial a place in, you'll have a very good feel for what to expect in terms of numbers; you'll also become skilled at knowing what part of the day's cycle the bite is in at a given time. That means if you've been averaging 20 recently, and you managed to land only 5 by noon today, you know the peak of activity is still ahead of you in the afternoon. On the other hand, if you are sitting on 17 by noon, you know they're on the verge of slowing down, and you may only have a good hour left before they die off. Again, this assumes you're going out pretty regularly. If not, you can still rely on the rule and wait them out while you work diligently to cover water.

Look no further than winter for those character building days on the water. It's now that a stillwater fly fisher can work on the finer points of his or her game (where ice-free conditions allow). Afternoon can be a relatively productive time to search for trout when winter comes calling.

Winter Afternoons. Often the warmest part of the day, this is when most or all activity will happen in winter. Don't count on that exclusively, but know that it occurs regularly. I'd love to be able to say that this is when they come out on days that are cold or slow, and you should just show up after lunch. But it doesn't work that way. You need every advantage you can get, including the full day of angling, when you can get it. But knowing afternoons are commonly more active *will* keep you on track and help you stay focused when it seems you've missed the train that day. And it may be the only thing that keeps you from throwing in the towel prematurely at times.

Along those lines, I can say I've spent a lot of full days on the water when it's anything but peak season, and the most common mistake I see anglers make is leaving too soon after a short outing with little or no luck.

No doubt it's really tough to justify staying out there when it's uncomfortably cold and the lake is slow. The thing to remember here is it may have been slow that part of the day, but as it turned out, the bite was right around the corner when you took off. Often I can set my watch by that part of midday when the launch gets busy with the first wave of anglers getting off the water because the morning was slow. About then you can start getting serious, because you know the bite is about to get going. I'll get more into human behavior in a minute, but this one is worth pointing out here since it happens so frequently. A simple change of habit would really pay off most days. In other words, it's an easy fix.

First Light/Last Light. These are usually short windows but very consistent. My best theory is that fish simply have the strong instinct to feed at these two parts of the day in low lighting. This allows them the stealth to be less visible to predators and to their own prey alike. In better weather, much activity can occur at these two times when a lot more food can be had. In winter, it seems they'll come out and take advantage of the same low-visibility situation whether food is present or not. Perhaps they'll come out for the purpose of safer searching. But whether there is food to be had or not, fish seem to be on the hunt, and I've found my offering at these times is usually well received. Overall, these don't tend to be the primary times for feeding in a day, but they make great bookends to an outing.

Your job is to recognize the potential and likelihood for a little action within these short windows and to focus your game on capitalizing. Think shoals and shorelines, since these are commonly good hunting grounds that offer both cover and food habitat. I usually prioritize the shoals first, and I may or may not get to the shorelines, depending on my success. And I'd say most of the time the shoals are it. Sometimes it's only a fish or two at each end, but over the course of a day, in slow conditions, this handful you hit at first and last light will add nicely to your total.

Put-in/Takeout. This one may be explained by the above, or it can be a variation on the same principle if you are fishing less than an entire day. Logic might not explain this one as well, since low lighting may not be a factor. But the pure and simple truth is, I've made it a habit for years and am regularly surprised by the results. Here you're taking more of a roll of the dice, but the reasoning still makes sense. For one thing, it's effective a surprising amount of the time. So even though good logic may be lacking, if the results are there, you just do it. I know I've said it before, but I don't need something to make sense if it puts fish into my net. If I'm benefitting from the unexplained behavior, that's good enough. My first priority is to capitalize; then, if I can figure it out, great. If I never do, fine. I still want those fish.

For another, it's a "free roll" of the dice, since you're already there and geared up. So you're not really sacrificing anything in terms of time. And to clarify, what I'm referring to here is simply working the immediate area where you put in and take out. That may be a boat launch, a roadside pull-out, or virtually anywhere you can jump into and out of the water. Much of the time, there's nothing special about these areas; you're just working them over because you happen to be there at two specific parts of the day. In other words, why not?

And any time I've drawn a strike doing this, I'll always try turning it into more strikes. In this way, that one lucky fish has, at times, turned into more—even into a significant part of my total for an outing. I also know a lot of anglers make this a habit out of simple fisherman's instinct, so I'm not claiming to introduce anything new here. But if this isn't a regular part of your routine, why not include it—it's free. Even if these ones are pure luck, take them. Again, it all adds up, and you're looking to turn over every possible rock on slow days. If this trick yields one fish every other outing on average (and that's pretty realistic), I'll gladly take it.

TECHNIQUES AND TIPS
You're Blind and It's Dark Out
We previously talked about how to cover water in a blind search—sectioning the lake off into five categories and then picking them apart, one by one, until action was found. To review, they were shoreline, shoal shallow, shoal deep, open shallow, and open deep. In colder conditions, morning in particular, I'd spend some extra time in those deeper sections along the outer shoals and in the open. And again, deep means 15 or so feet. I wouldn't go much beyond 20 feet in most cases if you're fishing deeper lakes. There are exceptions to that, but I'm referring to most of the water we fish. I'd limit the time I search shallower sections and along the shoreline in the earlier parts of the day, giving them just enough to determine any surprises. Then, later in the day, when fish finally start getting active, pay them a bit more attention. In slower parts of the year, you'll find yourself spending more time at this than you would in, say, late spring, when nearly everything seems to be hatching.

In these extended periods of little or no activity, you're just trying to hit the occasional fish—while also looking for the beginning of the day's action. So if I spend four hours in the morning doing a blind search and waiting for the bite to come on, one fish each hour would be just fine if I can make that happen. Let's say I only get one fish every two hours during this time. Again, fine. Just like those periods of first and last light, even a couple of fish will contribute nicely to the day's total.

By now, I'm sure you can see a pattern starting to develop regarding how fish can add up over the course of a slow day. It may happen painfully, a few at a time, but if you stay engaged at it and manage every bit of your time, that number at day's end will be the ridiculous total we were talking about.

Your Sinking Line and You

I know, it's a love-hate relationship, especially early on, when that floater casts so much easier and seems to hang in the air forever. This darn sinker always coils up, and you spend half your time untangling it. Then it casts awkwardly and feels funny in the water. The sinker really is good for nothing except deep trolling when nothing else works—I've heard it. I've lived it.

But in lake terms it's the equivalent of going from a bicycle to a car. At first that car is the most awkward and dangerous thing to undertake, and the bike was so simple and easy. The bike always got you where you were going, so who needs a car? Same logic here. In stillwater, you may see 10 percent of your potential with a floater if you work really hard and are lucky. But that's where it stops. If your ambition doesn't go beyond the schoolyard and the corner market up the street, by all means stay on the bike. You get the rest.

So for those of you who have held out as diehards with your floaters, this is pretty much the end of the line. Once you cross over and take an interest in more advanced stillwater angling, you can't master things like slower parts of the year, covering water effectively, exploiting opportunities, or other challenges without constant use of a full sink.

By now, if you've only started getting familiar with the full sink, or have refrained, while kicking and screaming, in favor of that lime green security blanket, it's not a lost cause. However, another new habit has to be formed before you can go any further. If it were possible, I'd instruct anyone new to stillwater to begin with a full sink, and to skip the floater until the first opportunity for a dry fly arises. But in the majority of cases, including my own, it just doesn't happen that way. The fact is, the floater is one of the biggest inhibitors to progress when learning this craft. Once more: Anglers who make use of sinkers are worlds apart from those who don't when it comes to lakes and ponds. What to do? If this sounds like you (that's OK), stop and take a short break from everything else fishing-related while you grab that sinker and become one with it. Spend entire days with it, and get used to catching fish on it. The process won't take long, and once complete, plan on using it 95 percent of the time from then on. I literally use my floater for dry flies, and that's about it. It's a different story on moving water, but on stillwater, the full sink is king. Remember, you've been riding a bicycle; where you're going, you'll need a car.

Managing a Hotspot

It's been several hours, and, so far, all that patience and perseverance haven't exactly worn a hole in your net. Next thing you know, they've all come in to occupy that shallow weedy section of shoreline at the far end of the lake. No clue why, you just know they're in there, lots of them, from a sampling of casts. Fortunately, you paid attention to that first strike and stuck around, which led you to the discovery. You might eventually figure out the reason for the gathering, but right now it's your job to capitalize. You may even find the intensity of strikes increases after you hit a few.

A find like this is a little more difficult to manage than one where the food source is obvious. In those cases, you work the cycle of the hatch or occurrence, whereas here, you're not really sure how long the gathering will last. In a small, defined area like this section of shoreline, I'll simply stay on it till the strikes quit coming. Sometimes a spot like this will yield 5 or 6, while at other times it may yield a number closer to 20. It can be anything. Once the strikes stop, I usually give it just enough time to make sure it's done—usually a few minutes is plenty—then move away and let it cool off a while.

And unless you've found another great opportunity right afterward (not likely on a slow day), give it 20 or 30 minutes and then come back. It doesn't always work, but I can usually squeeze a fished-out hotspot for another couple of fish if I go back. Then again, at times these spots will light right back up once they've had a rest. A fished-out hotspot still makes for a good opportunity and may well be your best at that particular time. So always return and try to recapitalize. If it produces anything on that second round, even one, repeat the process again—moving away, and coming back in time.

How often should you go back? Until you finally get blanked. So you may end up going back only once, or as many as several times. Either way, a good hotspot in slow conditions is a major find, and that single event might make your entire outing.

Missed Strikes. On the miss, always go right back at it, same cast. That gives you the biggest odds for hookup on the next throw. A surprisingly high percentage of missed strikes will take again on the next try. In most cases, your fish is still there, and I always find that he wants what he just missed. That's the behavior, anyway. Same on an early retrieve miss. Don't instantly pull out to recast. Just keep retrieving all the way back, and a lot of them will resume the chase. Browns are famous for this.

Short Strikes. Beyond new or sharp hooks, I like going to patterns that leave a well-exposed hook, such as the Ruby Eyed Leech, Six Pack, or Goat Hair Leech, where the body, or hook shaft area, has a low profile. The standard Carey Special, Wooly Bugger, or Olive Willy are examples of ones I don't care for as much in this circumstance, since the bodies tend to be thicker. If you're counting on just catching that outer lip, it probably matters. In any case, it helps my confidence, which matters just as much.

When short-striking is prevalent, a common method of setting the hook is the "strip-strike" approach—in which a short, deliberate tug of the line is used instead of raising the rod tip. For another, even more subtle, approach, I'll freeze altogether on the take (rod tip is already submerged), hold a moment while I can feel the fish and then slowly raise the tip. It's almost a non-hook set, but it works, and it keeps you from pulling through an already delicate hook position. Your work is cut out for you at that point, but at least he's on.

Fish that short-strike and then are feisty on the play can be next to impossible to keep on. You can up your odds quite a bit by using one other highly effective trick: submerging the rod tip as deep as you can (point it straight down), and playing the fish underwater. Not foolproof, but it changes your line dynamics completely—and gives the fish a lot less wiggle room to work with. They won't break surface as much, and when they do, they have only a foot or two of exposed line to shake; they'd have 30 or 40 feet from your raised tip. I've found this technique to be a little too effective, so much so that it feels a bit like cheating. However, when they get

Low lighting and fog are among those less obvious clues that may signal increased activity.

that stubborn, I might go to it as a last resort. Since this method is not as much fun, and it's not exactly a tournament out there, I don't use it much. Nice having it up my sleeve though.

Remember the Less Obvious Clues
In the absence of visible activity or food sources, remember to watch for the more abstract occurrences that may still give away the timing and location of fish. On any abrupt weather change, look for activity to begin or pick up. Pay special attention to a change that reduces lighting or other forms of visibility.

Also, you'll recall that wind can have a lot of influence, and can even act like cover in some cases. Check near any artificial seams created on the lake surface, as well as against windswept sections of shoreline where bottom and shallow surface are stirred up. Again, this may provide a noticeable combination of cover and exposed food for trout. Often, those hotspots we were discussing are created by this situation.

Shade is another good place to search, especially when a single end of the lake is the only place not exposed to direct sunlight. Like the other clues mentioned, it's not a sure bet. But when you're coming up blank, and there are no signs of life, it's probably the most obvious next move. Also, remember our previous discussion about watching other anglers.

If the Skunk Still Comes Calling

Forget feeling the pressure here. At times, your execution in slow conditions will be near flawless. Yet, as the day wears on fishless, you'll begin having those thoughts of "what if." Here's another opportunity for you to demonstrate what an experienced angler does. We don't control the availability of these fish; we can only play a good game in search of them. And when you know you've played well, the pressure is off.

Instead of feeling frustrated, recognize the value of the game you're going to play between now and takeout. In this circumstance, you'll have the opportunity to try things you otherwise would not resort to, and that's when a lot of very useful skills are learned for the first time. Creative search methods, perseverance, growing a thicker skin, and other valuable tools can be developed for you to use and benefit from later on.

Two things you always want to do beyond that: Leave no stone uncovered in a day, and, if the outing ends fishless, keep fishing mentally after you leave by trying to figure out what may have worked. What else could you have tried, or what things can you still learn that you have not yet tried? Was there an end of the lake that you overlooked? Was there a time of day that you weren't on the water; for example, did you arrive later in the morning or at midday? Did you cover all the depths, and did you vary your presentations and retrieves? Were other anglers out there, and how did they do? If you saw anyone else catch fish, what all did you observe about the circumstances? You get the point. Many times, I may exhaust all possibilities while on the water. But after the fact, when I have more time to think, the ideas will start flowing again. Make sure you allow this to happen. In fact, I'd do this even after a good outing. Much of what you can learn will happen between outings, as you go through the problem-solving process in your head.

MORE ON WINTER

Along with being less comfortable on the water, expect to catch a lot less fish in winter. The colder temperatures will make fish relatively inactive,

The thought of getting into a float tube and sitting waist deep in 40-degree water may sound uninviting, but it still beats a day at the mall anytime.

and food sources aren't as plentiful either. Look for them to hold where the warmer layers sit in the water column. Consider the trends in the weather, as the "warm spot" could be down deep or near surface. This depends on the general direction of temperatures outside. Regardless, you're usually best to search high and low each time out; let them show you where they feel like holding that day. And since most action is usually in that first 15 feet or so, you don't need to do a lot of experimenting with depths, especially in light of field-of-vision considerations. I still think they see a lot more than we give them credit for, and you don't have to exactly match the depth where they hold in order to get their attention.

Timing. Look for them to get active during the warmer parts of the day. Late morning and early afternoon are often good bets. I've also seen spikes in feeding at first and last light; these tend to be short-lived but are usually good for a small handful. Also, pay attention to warming trends during midwinter. Fish will react to changes in temperature and other conditions, regardless of the month they take place in. I've seen fall happen in January, and spring happen in February, when weather has been unseasonably warm. As a rule of thumb, anytime the weather makes a leap toward the middle from either direction (let's call 55 degrees F the middle), I go fishing. In my experience, trout always react favorably to weather that spikes toward 55 degrees and will often hit the shallower depths to feed.

   Method. You'll hear a lot about using a slow approach: slow, deep trolling for example. That's certainly not wrong when fish hold down low

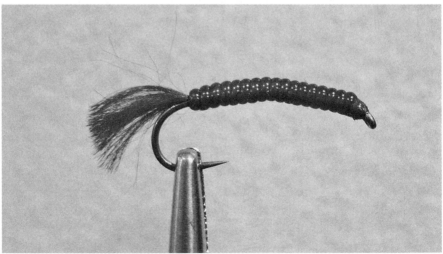

Two winter favorites: Halfback Nymph, Bloodworm.

and are conserving energy; however, I would advise against making a generalization there. As with any other time of year, consider first the big picture, and make the best approach based on all the relevant factors. Say you're out on New Year's Day. The fact that your calendar says January 1 won't mean anything to the fish. The current weather trend, the temperatures of surface and other layers relative to each other, time of day, light intensity, wind or degree of surface chop, availability and location of food, and a slew of other factors will determine WHEN and WHERE those fish will be found. And that could be anywhere on January 1. Now, say the weather has been spring-like since Christmas, and food exists high up in the water column. Your game might actually be a shallow, faster retrieve, and that's not uncommon in winter. In one day, I might use three or four different approaches, just depending on where I find action. Again, keep an open mind out there (while you struggle to stay warm).

Patterns. I really don't do anything special just because it is winter or it's cold. January has never given me reason to abandon my trusty leech. Truth be known, you could probably fish it all winter and do just fine. In fact, I'd venture that more folks go to this fly in the cold. Beyond that, I would advise selecting patterns in the same way you would at any other time of year—open mind, read the situation, and make your best decision. Other examples: Chironomid fishers tend to do quite well on bloodworm patterns fished near the lake floor. In clear conditions, I might go to a smaller profile pattern for general searching. The neutral appearance of a Halfback Nymph works just fine. And if you like a certain fly that may be out of season for purposes of imitation, try it anyway. I can think of a few good patterns that would officially represent damsels, but which work as well as anything at the "wrong" time of year. Again, trout don't care nearly as much as we do. We like to overthink everything; they don't.

THE HEAT OF SUMMER
All lakes are not created equal. While some may slow down during warmer periods, others might come on nicely for bass or warmwater fish, and still others will just continue producing trout with good energy. Lakes with more depth, cover, abundant foods, or even a locational advantage (e.g., near the saltwater, at elevation, or in a steep draw) are commonly less affected by warmer weather. And just like *winter, summer* can take on a number of different meanings, depending on which region you live or fish in.

Rate of Temperature Change. At any temperature, trout have the most adverse reaction to abrupt, significant change. That means the current *trend* affects behavior much more than the current *temperature*. With enough time, they can adapt to most conditions, but they really don't like a sudden change of any kind.

Bottom Line. As previously mentioned, while energetic fish can often be found in warmer parts of the year, give them a rest if they start coming up tired.

HUMAN BEHAVIOR

We've studied fish behavior quite a bit by now, but common behavior among anglers is also a very useful topic. We'll look at it here in the context of slow conditions, and then look at it again in the discussion on favorable conditions. The basic question is which of the common actions or behaviors displayed on the water are best avoided. And I'm not referring to rude or unsocial behavior in any way. Rather, I'm talking about the things anglers do that don't put them on fish. Understand that most or all of these behaviors are normal, not because the angler was ignorant or necessarily inexperienced. Still, the discussion is well worth having, since we can easily learn from it.

Late Arrival/Early Dismissal. This can't be avoided a lot of the time. The way life works, you go fishing when you can—and much of the time that's not all day. To the extent that you are able, I highly recommend putting in a full day on the water. When the bite is tough, this will up your odds by a lot. I've seen countless anglers show up or leave at the wrong time, only to miss the action by a mere hour or two.

Running Them Over. Much more common than you might think. It's easy to place yourself where your casts should be landing. Over shallow parts of a shoal, or up against the shoreline, always consider where fish may likely be holding. Could they be further out from shore than you think? Usually, if I believe the fish are in tight, I'll still work the outward area before I go in closer. And sure enough, probably half of the time I end up drawing strikes where I had intended to sit or pass over. Along shore, always present from out and away instead of trolling right up against. We talked about this before, but I can't emphasize it enough. Rowing or kicking over the top of anything in two to three-feet of water is simply poor execution.

Constant Fly Change. By now, if you still think changing out your fly will change your luck, think again. I watch a surprising number of anglers do this all day—to no avail—while ignoring all the things that will actually make a difference. If you're not drawing strikes, you won't attract fish by simply selecting the right fly. You need to go find them. WHEN and WHERE come first, or forget it.

Supersizing. There is a time and a place for going big, but it isn't that often. Even the largest trout in the lake will pass on a large pattern when conditions aren't right. On more than one occasion, I have advised folks to size down and then watched them get instant results from it. Whereas you can't attract fish by simply offering the right fly, you certainly can chase them away by throwing too much of one at them.

All That Lime Green. Truth is, on a day when only a full sink should be used, I always see more floaters on the water. If I had to guess, probably two-thirds of a lake's crowd will have them on a day when active fish are located at depth. And what's worse, there aren't many days during the year when you should use one. Excessive use of floaters is another very common reason people get skunked.

Dying on a Rock. This means staying with a method that isn't producing, without ever moving on. We have a tendency to remain in our proverbial comfort zone, even when abandonment becomes the obvious choice. Any time you have success with some method, be mindful that it worked under a certain set of conditions, and that nothing is universal. Raise the question every half-hour of nonproductive time.

Camping. This is the same concept as dying on a rock, only with respect to location. It may have produced one fish, eight fish, or maybe it produced last weekend, but when that hole dries up, it's time to move on. Once you're camping, you're no longer fishing.

One Cast and a Thousand Kicks. Nothing is universal, especially not trolling. Trust me—you're not covering water like you think you are.

Joined at the Hip. Nothing wrong with good friends fishing together; I do it regularly. Again, just make sure you split up and fish the way you normally would. Side-by-side is a great way to hang out but a lousy way to cover water.

Bliss. This one happens a lot and is tough to watch. In the face of overwhelming clues, other anglers having big success, or even an eyeful of visible activity on the surface, a lot of anglers simply don't see it. Or some will just stick to their unproductive methods, refusing to change up in favor of something that is obviously working at the moment. If you ask me, observing and reacting are the most interesting things we do as anglers. Without these as part of the experience, I'd probably quit out of boredom.

Staying Home. The off-season certainly has its share of stay-at-home days, but they're much fewer than you might think. At times when the action was surprisingly good, I've had places to myself, or shared with only one or two others—simply because it was raining or cold. Even algae can chase away a lot of would-be anglers who don't care for the color green, yet the bite often heats up underneath that top layer of pea soup. Beyond extreme weather, or the combination of cold and wind that makes for miserable or dangerous conditions, I always opt to show up. If I fish 80 to 100 times per year, probably 20 to 30 of those are days when most others have chosen to stay home and left a perfectly good outing on the table. I suppose I should say thank you.

Narrow Horizons. Similar to staying home, this means limiting your geographic horizons while on the water. Just because everyone else is staying at the convenient end of the lake, that doesn't mean you should join them. If it makes sense to locate there, by all means do. Otherwise I'd venture out and cover the areas that most likely hold fish. All too often, all the anglers are at one end of the lake while all the fish are at the other end.

The Routine. This could be a method such as trolling, or it could be a location, or it could be anything else you repeat every time out. My advice is to avoid ruts as best you can, even if it seems unproductive at first. The above description of "bliss" closely relates here. Strict routines only serve as a big limitation, yet I see them all the time. If the chain of events in your outing is no different than it was last time, or at any other time, something is wrong. On the other hand, if no two of your outings are ever the same, that's the first sign you're doing it right.

Not Speaking Up. I understand the logic here. I've done it myself lots of times. Someone is having big success out there, and I'm not. If I can't figure it out by observation, the smartest thing I can do is go right up and start asking questions. I know, easier than it sounds. That requires breaking some ice and being social. But I still think it's less painful than continuing to get blanked while another guy bangs them out right in front of me. I've seldom heard of anyone getting snubbed for doing this. On the contrary, it's one of the best forms of flattery, and anyone hitting fish like that is highly likely to be in a good mood. And from the other side, the only thing better than catching a lot of fish is helping others do it. My advice is, speak up and look forward to the day when others come to you. It isn't far off.

ADDING IT ALL UP

It's been a long day, and they weren't exactly jumping into your net. Let's see how you did. Granted, you could do everything right in a day and still end up skunked, or land 20-something by the time you get out. It all comes back to the hand you're dealt. But you can still play that hand to its fullest, and that's exactly what we're after here. To help visualize how it typically goes, we'll break the day down by opportunity and measure the results.

Recon/Trends. It certainly isn't the best time of year, and recent outings saw most of the action centered on midday. First light has been worth showing up for and is producing better than last light, where one or two are considered good. No visible food sources, not for quite a while, and the majority of strikes are coming at depth, with outer shoals being a pretty good bet. Shoreline has been spotty at best, some days yielding only a fish or two. Not many anglers have been showing lately, and activity among them has been limited.

Today's Weather/Temperatures. Chilly and overcast, with mild rain and light winds expected. Should be stable for the most part, so likely weather won't be much of a factor. Low: 36 degrees F. High: 45 degrees F. Surface: 43 degrees F.

First Light (3 fish). You put in before daybreak. A few casts near the launch and nothing, so you move across to a nearby shoal to set up for first light. That first hour and a half you get some action, although limited. You draw a handful of takes at depth along the outer shoal. Sure enough, they're hitting funny; you need to resort to a stickier fly and very soft hook sets. By the time it shuts down, you've landed three.

Morning Stretch (2 fish). The next three hours go by painfully slowly. You manage to hit one along shore, with no luck finding repeat business. The only other one comes by "accident" while you are moving downshore at a troll. Fine, those count. Two other missed strikes, and that's it for the morning. Two more landed for your efforts. Seems discouraging to go this length of time with so little action, but remember, most anglers out there will end the entire day with only a couple of fish.

Noon (4 fish). A good strike along shore finally wakes you up. You look at your watch and wonder if the action could finally pick up. A little attention paid to the same section brings another strike, and then another.

These fish seem to be serious about feeding. OK, it's official; you've run across some kind of hotspot. As it turns out, you've seen better, but considering the day, this will certainly do. After landing four, the spot goes cold. You move on with the thought of coming back in a half-hour or so. Turns out the spot died for good, but still add those four to your total.

Early Afternoon (5 fish). Although your hotspot died down after just a few fish, you seem to be gaining momentum into the afternoon. You're finding strikes at a little depth, not in big numbers, but they're consistent. While the opportunity is here you decide to postpone lunch until things slow back down. Good move, going hungry got you another 5 to the net before it cooled off.

Late Lunch. You're used to it by now, as the action has come on around lunchtime for the last several weeks. The trend has also told you that the next couple of hours or so will produce next to nothing, so no hurry on finishing lunch. Your time is likely better spent taking a break and getting warm.

Late Afternoon (1 fish). Sure enough, they don't exactly come running when you get back into the water. One more, by accident, as you move along the shoreline, but forget making it repeat.

Evening/Last Light (2 fish). By the time some evidence of life comes back, you have about an hour to make good. Two more to the net, and that's it.

Takeout (1 fish). You have a 10-minute commute back to the launch, where one more accident happens while trolling. That's the last for today, as a few casts around the launch prove unfruitful. By now, you're not as concerned about that as you are about getting out, getting warm, and getting home for dinner.

Let's add it up: $3 + 2 + 4 + 5 + 1 + 2 + 1 = 18$

Eighteen is a seemingly unheard-of number on a day when most anglers are staying home from slow fishing, and those who do show up are lucky to take a fish or two. In fact, a lot of anglers won't hit a number like this on the active days. Yet it's no fluke, and you can count on doing it next time, as well. No rocket science, no magic, no secret pattern—you're just fishing differently now, adhering to a simple set of principles throughout the day. You now understand where the limited opportunities will likely be, how to recognize them, and how best to take advantage of them. You'll spend the majority of the day getting blanked like everyone else, but you

Winter morning on Lone Lake, Whidbey Island, Washington.

have the ability to find those few chances unrecognized by most, and you can now exploit them to the fullest. Along with that, you'll end up working harder, thinking harder, and probably spending more time on the water than others that day. It doesn't come for free, but if you ask me, that's where the sport is.

We began this entire discussion by studying timing and placement as the primary drivers for catching fish. We talked about finding the most productive waters, and then, once on those lakes, finding fish. And while you may find the best fishing by getting these first two principles (WHEN and WHERE) right, there is tremendous value in seeking out more challenging situations instead of staying home to wait for better conditions. Simply put, you will develop a lot further as an angler by confronting and working through those subpar days on the water. You'll have the privilege of facing tough circumstances, and you'll find ways to get results despite the odds.

You'll become confident, even tough, with a fly rod, and will also find yourself taking a lot more fish than expected when the action heats back up. My advice: Fish as often as you can, all year long, and you'll get plenty of experience at swinging the odds your way when it otherwise doesn't look so good.

Now let's see what happens when these principles are applied on more active days. Try not to have too much fun!

Lesson 7

STRATEGIES FOR ACTIVE DAYS

When the tables are turned and the lake is full of good clues and activity—problem solved. Or is it? Remember the idea of seeing clues in a new way, and exploiting good opportunities every time they present themselves? This kind of puzzle now presents a new and better challenge for you as an advanced fly fisher. Instead of enjoying an easy 8 or 10 fish day, you'll begin practicing methods that may yield closer to 40 or 50—maybe more—in that same outing. Sounds like a pipe dream at first, but consider the result of a strong working knowledge of trout behavior, combined with your ability to take full advantage of a day filled with abundant opportunities. In the right conditions, active fish can be found most of the day—sometimes all day—and staying on them for that long will multiply the kind of results most are used to. Activity will likely fluctuate over the course of the day but, if you're able to make use of the cards dealt in each hour, the end result is usually a pretty big number.

One more reminder: Believe it or not, there can be too much of a good thing when fish are this active. Fish count is certainly a way to measure results and the effectiveness of your techniques, but don't forget the real endgame here. We're out there to have fun, and that should always be where the value is. When an outing starts to become more work and less fun, it's time to dial it down. You may be trying too hard, or even catching too many fish. In any case, let's examine what might lead to that problem. Here we'll look at principles from the previous discussion on slow conditions, along with other principles that just apply on active days.

Once again, becoming familiar with a small handful of good lakes and ponds will pay handsomely here. By learning a body of water intimately, you'll know its terrain inside and out and, more importantly, dial in to its various food sources. You'll be familiar with their cycles, the priority each of them takes among fish, and how you can best take advantage. You'll figure out the timing, placement, and methods that will keep your net the most active, as well as recognizing all those subtle and delicate details that keep you on fish in the midst of constant change.

One of the most useful tools an angler can possess is the ability to recognize, understand, and follow change as it happens. Otherwise, that run of luck you had working a midge hatch on Sunday will only leave you stumped the following Saturday when you excitedly rush back to capitalize on the same situation. Only now, the situation has mysteriously changed, and those two dozen rainbows you were counting on are nowhere to be found. Most likely they're still taking midges, but a lot can happen in six days. A new weather system came in midweek, the timing of peak hatch was altered, and most of the fish are just lying low till that three-hour period when feeding will be easiest and most plentiful. And to top it off, they're more scattered now, so you won't be able to work a small area, drawing strikes every third cast.

This is the kind of constant change that not only defines our sport, but makes it interesting; it provides the angler with a new and unique puzzle every time out. So when your dream circumstance from last weekend gets shot to pieces, it doesn't mean something bad has happened. It means you get to solve a new puzzle, and you won't be getting bored at it any time soon. I'm always grateful for this constant state of flux, and for the chaos of a thousand overturned puzzle pieces that need to be arranged into an orderly solution.

Along those lines, I think the best part of any good hatch is the cycle, or progressive evolution, that it presents over the course of several weeks. In this way, a single food source—and the way trout partake of it—will continually change, thus presenting a whole series of challenging puzzles to be solved during this time. Following this natural progression of change, along with continuing to fish the hatch effectively, makes for some of the most interesting and rewarding parts of stillwater fly fishing for trout. And once again, the answers can have little or nothing to do with the fly you select. As always, you're striving to understand changes in behavior among fish and then to place yourself in the middle of them—at the right time and place, with a method of presentation that caters to their current frame of mind. And to continue sounding like a broken record—get this far, and it

An alpine lake in summer is the perfect setting for a career day on the water. Remember your thermals, as elevated lakes may still be subject to winter-like water temperatures, even at this time of year. I learned that the hard way.

won't matter what you put on a hook in front of them. Just present it and hang on; you're in for a career day.

TIMING AND YOUR SCHEDULE

As you become familiar with the various food sources for trout—along with optimal weather conditions, and the more productive parts of the year (typically spring and fall when temperatures are mild)—you can clear your schedule accordingly to take full advantage. Putting yourself on known opportunities, and allowing time to dial them in, will do more than just help you catch a lot of fish. You'll spend enough time with a food source, or with a portion of a season, to observe the various behavior and nuances that occur throughout.

This process of learning, problem solving, and technique revision will eventually take much of the guesswork out of following change and understanding cycles. You'll be able to interpret new observations based on experience, and as each change occurs, you'll know what the most effective course of action is. You'll also develop a good sense for windows of opportunity, their timelines, and how to best manage them. And for my money, whenever something big or extraordinary happens for an angler, it was all about timing.

BUYING IN

Just as before, your level of confidence will fuel everything else you bring to the table. The first step in any successful outing, whether it's dead or overwhelmingly active, is to go in believing, or buying in. Remember our discussion on fly choice, and your belief or disbelief in a particular pattern? No matter which fly you use, your success with any pattern will hinge on your level of confidence as you present it. In the very same way, your level of confidence will show itself in everything else you do, from put-in to take-out. For me, it starts with the prospect of failure and *what if*. Once I'm OK with any result, good or bad, I'm free to fish hard, with an open mind and full focus on making the best of everything that occurs that day. Funny how it works: I'm carefree regarding failure or getting skunked, and when it happens, I don't mind in the least. Yet it practically never happens (knock on wood).

Once you put 100 percent of your energy into success, and can live with any failure that may occur, the failure part just quits happening on its own. And if it ever rears its head, who cares? Besides, we have control over true failure. If you and I choose to learn from a skunking or a dismal outing, and come back better next time, how is that failure? In short, if you go in believing, set yourself free of concern for failure, and devote all your thought and energy to the opportunities at hand, you've already won. All that's left is enjoying whatever happens, and helping others out there.

ABUNDANT CLUES

While at slower times of the year, you'll spend most or all of the day in blind search mode, in this situation, you'll be able to connect the dots with a good number of visible clues from start to finish. At times you'll even have more than one to choose from, and it's your job to prioritize them and put yourself where the greatest concentrations are likely to be. In a single moment you can spot a handful of anglers in different locations, using different methods, all catching fish. Usually personal preference will determine the chosen method of each. For example, one angler may prefer to fish Chironomids from a stationary position, while another works the open water with a sinking line and streamer in constant movement. Both can be equally effective at the same time. The key here is still putting yourself where active fish are, effectively drawing strikes regardless of the method you select.

I tend to choose my own methods by a combination of personal preference and results. What usually interests me most is observing and understanding trout behavior at a given time and then choosing the most effective approach to address it. If I can accomplish that with a fly that doesn't belong to the time of year, or match the food source, that's even better. At every possible turn, I attempt to prove that fish are not lured by simple imitation. Rather, I seek to attract trout by locating them, understanding what affects their behavior, and then executing an approach that draws a reaction based on that behavior.

In my experience, most of the time trout don't show up to eat damsels or midges specifically. They just show up to eat, period. And you'll most likely find them where food exists. With little exception, they'll take anything with the appearance of a possible meal, and ask questions later. If it turns out to be something other than food, they'll simply spit it out. It may even be a biological reflex that occurs independently of any rational thought.

Whatever the reason, it's fine with me. By the time they take it, it's too late for them; I've already set the hook. Again, not imitating is just my

Just one of a number of clues known to appear in more active periods, this damsel is a sign well worth investigating.

preference. Most anglers enjoy, and even believe in, imitation as the best way to go, and consider it an important part of the sport. These two schools of thought, along with others, can coexist in stillwater fly fishing simply as different forms of preference. My form of preference seeks to understand what matters most in drawing trout, in order of relevance—thus the idea of WHEN–WHERE–HOW–WHAT. In so doing, I'm attempting to get rid of as many limitations as I can by prioritizing the things that matter most to a trout. Imitation is fine, until it draws an angler away from these priorities and curtails his or her success. I see it every time out. More on this in a minute.

WHAT'S GOING ON

Another game changer. Beyond following a given set of clues in a day, experienced anglers will have a fairly complete understanding of the waters they fish in terms of the various food sources, when they occur, and how they cycle. In each year, the timing, duration, and relative abundance of food sources will occur uniquely from any other year; however, you can still count on them taking place every season. With a good working knowledge of the waters you fish, you'll know roughly when to expect the various insects and other foods, as well as how to spot the early signs as they approach. The idea here, once again, is to spend regular time on your lakes and ponds of choice, and to become familiar with what the trout feed on throughout the year. In a single year, you can get a good feel for what occurs there. In maybe three years of regular visits, you should be able start making good predictions of upcoming events, and to react well to them with a fly rod. That means observing the feeding behavior of trout as each food source occurs and cycles through, and developing an understanding of what goes on beneath the surface.

In time you'll have a good grip on the unseen, based on your knowledge and experience with food sources and the current set of visible clues. This understanding will, in turn, drive the decisions you make about WHEN, WHERE, and HOW to look for fish throughout the year. And, as you can imagine, the variety of clues you encounter throughout a day will no longer come as a surprise. From your understanding of what's going on, you'll expect most of the clues you'll come across when you show up on any given day.

A final note, much of this knowledge of food sources will apply across most lakes in your area—a major midge hatch in early spring, or damsels in

Forget first and most: Aaron Whitson goes straight for the win with the biggest fish of the day. With great effort, I managed to come in second. Problem is there were only two of us fishing!

the summer—and you can use it to explore new waters with a great deal of success. Just note that each body of water also has its own unique set of fingerprints that distinguish it from anyplace else. And getting familiar with those fingerprints will put you on exponentially more fish, time after time, as you frequent a single lake.

THAT DREADED SINKER AGAIN

Just as your full sink was a required tool for navigating slow conditions, you'll need it equally as much to capitalize when times are good. It's common practice to use the floater when there is a lot of visible activity at the surface, yet in most cases, fish are still not taking food right on top. You may observe insects or other foods afloat, and even see disturbance from the fish themselves, but until you witness a fair number of them rising to surface fare, you're usually best off with a subsurface line (Chironomid rigs notwithstanding). Most anglers prefer more than one sinking line, so you might use a Type II, for example, to fish beneath the surface but higher up in the water column.

In any case, the more you make the move toward full sinking lines in stillwater, the more fish you'll put yourself on. And any time you're using a floater for something other than dry fly presentation, or for running Chironomids at depth via long leader, I would pay a lot of attention to your success rate in drawing strikes. If you've nailed WHEN and WHERE down for sure, and are still missing the action, consider it your first and best clue that line choice is an issue. Same goes for a sinking tip line. If you ask me, they serve very limited purpose on lakes at best, and may very well serve no purpose. All of mine are used for moving water only, and they do tend to work tremendously well there. The good news is, you and I are here to catch fish, not to make the longest or prettiest casts, so the trade-off is always worth it. Trust me: On the coolness scale, fish-on trumps a pretty cast every time. Floater for dries; Chironomid rigs and the occasional nymph near surface; full sink for everything else in stillwater—you won't go wrong.

WHEN TECHNIQUE AND STRATEGY ARE EVERYTHING

So far, so good. Conditions are ripe; you have a good command on current food sources and their respective cycles; you know WHEN and WHERE fish are most likely to be active; and you're now armed and confident with that full sink. However, a lot can still go wrong between your cast and setting the hook. In any form of fly fishing, the angler who ends the day with unusually good results, time after time, has mastered a number of very subtle techniques on the water. And stillwater fly fishing is certainly no exception.

Many of these details and techniques will go unnoticed by an outside observer, yet the results they bring to the net are unmatched and, in this sport, cannot be obtained by any other means. Your ability to execute on these finer points will develop over time, as you invest a lot of effort and practice. It's the only way I know of to gain that kind of skill. Whenever you see an angler taking an unusual number compared to everyone else, and nothing seems different about his methods, these fine points are invariably why. You simply cannot see the number of hours spent ahead of time in order to get to that point. Chances are this angler has put in an amount of time equal to everyone else's time combined. In that volume of time, an angler will mold his technique and approach in a lot of subtle ways, some of which develop and are employed with little or no conscious thought. They just happen "on their own"—with experience.

This dimension of your skill will continue to evolve as you put the hours in, so you're not looking to obtain a single, tangible level of ability. It's no different than learning to play a musical instrument. The longer you play, the better you get at it—but there is no end. You can just keep getting better and learning more over a lifetime, all the while enjoying the successes along the way. In fly fishing, some of those less obvious details will play a surprisingly large part in your success, or lack thereof, in a day, even when the lake boils over with activity. Let's talk about some of them.

Basic Execution

This can be a tough one to understand at first. I tend to think of it like pitching a baseball, where the simple act is easy enough to comprehend, but doing it with any success requires a lot of time developing just the right touch. With enough repetition, in time, your brain and arm will sync up and work together in unison. Your presentation on the water will evolve the same way, as you put in the hours of practice. Again, these will be largely unseen subtleties about the way your fly lands, sits, and moves, but it won't go unnoticed on the other end. The same can be said for spinners, spoons, and any other form of artificial bait used to lure fish. What gives it a natural or desirable appearance in the water is the work of your hands, not the simple appearance of it.

You'll need the knowledge and experience to select the best approach, but, once you make that decision, your hands still need the touch to pull it off just right. On the lake surface, it may be the way your fly lands and lays out; underneath, it might be your retrieve. Other casting skills like placement and wind negotiation are also important but are developed in less time and matter far less in drawing strikes. For our purpose here, I'm referring mostly to presentation.

We previously talked about seeing the fly underwater with your hands and giving it lifelike movement and appearance (see pages 71–72). Same idea here, only now we're applying this concept in very active water, where this small detail about your execution can be the difference between hitting a few and fully capitalizing on multiple times to hit many. When it comes to this kind of execution, I wish I could simply describe the action and have you turn right around and do it. But it really is like playing an instrument: The real work begins after the instruction, and many painstaking hours are spent in practice before getting it right. When I was a new fly fisher, I can recall this as being the most challenging and frustrating part to learn. I remember the anglers around me doing just fine hooking up, while I continuously got blanked doing what I thought was the exact same stuff—same setup, same fly, same depth, same everything. Or so I thought.

Beyond the submerged rod tip, you can't tell by sight whether the execution here is any good or not. Perhaps the only way to spot it is when fish are active. Then good execution shows itself by the amount of time spent hooked up.

I also remember getting the same advice from each of them, and it was very good advice: Don't worry, just keep at it, and the rest will work itself out. They were right. It did. And it's the very advice I would turn around and give someone now. Along with that, the best tip I can offer is to key-in on your strikes, and to pay a lot of attention to the movement of the fly and of your hands that lead up to each.

Covering Water Thoroughly

Even when the lake shows endless promise, you'll still live and die by your ability to cover water diligently and to take advantage of all that activity. Beyond an effective presentation on every cast, you need to put a reasonable number of those casts in front of fish. This means you must cover the water in your immediate vicinity without bypassing the majority of available opportunity. Seems obvious, but if you stop and think about it, anglers make that mistake all the time when the water is active. It's very easy to keep passing up good viable water in pursuit of what lies another few yards away, where you just saw two good rises in a row. That visual stimulation has the natural tendency to override good logic. It draws an angler in much the same way you and I are trying to draw a reaction from fish. When I know the immediate area holds good promise of unseen fish, I always try to think twice before taking that bait. Whether along the bank, across the shoals, or out in the open, you'll want to make the best use of your time by making as many well-thought-out casts, or presentations, as you can.

For example, in open water, the pie-shaped search outlined on page 113 is an effective way to cover the area that surrounds you. With each circle completed, you'll move the distance of approximately two casts in a logical direction and repeat the drill. And, as you probably remember, the amount of time you devote to this activity will be determined by the strikes it produces (or fails to produce). You're trying to ride that fine line between inching along too meticulously and carelessly skipping around. So the idea here is to pick up as many strikes as possible in the least amount of area covered, thus making the best use of your time. And to accomplish this, you'll need to put yourself on the most concentrated parts of the lake.

Finding Concentrations

Think back to that two-dimensional search we were talking about earlier. When seeking out concentrations of fish, you can look in terms of both time and location. On active days, you'll still find parts of the day that are busier than others. There can be several busy times, or even just one, with the lake still providing an abundance of action in a day. *Callibaetis* and damsel hatches are good examples of how a single part of the day produces most of the activity; the fish population just waits for the hatch to occur, since the food source can be so prolific. Then, at the other parts of the day, the fish simply rest up and conserve energy. The thing to know here is, at any given time, a lake's population of fish will be concentrated in some way or another. It makes sense, as conditions would never cater to an even distribution throughout a lake's acreage and depths. At times it may seem the fish are scattered, and we often describe the bite this way.

However, even if you find them spread out across the lake—for example, taking midges—they'll still be concentrated at a certain depth, depending on factors such as hatch cycle, layer temperatures, and surface visibility. Putting yourself on these concentrations may be a bit of a trick, even on the most active days. Obviously, this goes back to intimately knowing the waters you fish, and having good trend information from prior recent outings. But there also are a few ways to search them out in real time. Fortunately, it's anything but rocket science.

First, refer back to all the visual signs on the water. Is food or fish showing in any one place more than others? Sounds insultingly simple, but it's surprising what looking around will do—and even more surprising how many anglers miss the obvious signs of concentrated activity. Make sure your eyes get a good workout all day, or you'll never realize how much you're missing. I tend to give myself a sore neck from looking around the whole time when I fish. But if you ask me, the most productive anglers are the ones who constantly watch two things: the time, and the lake surface in all directions.

Another method of finding concentrated fish is by using the tool you already have in your hands—your fly rod. Your rod makes a very good indicator of activity when used with some confidence. I simply play hot/cold with the strikes I'm drawing until I zero in on the hotspot. And if it shifts, I just play the same game to try and follow it. Once again, insultingly simple, but who cares when it's that deadly?

When present, swallows make a very good indicator of fish concentration. This clue shows itself often in the better months and is usually prevalent in a strong midge hatch, or when mayflies pop in good numbers. Well worth observing, swallows may display similarities in behavior to that of feeding fish just below them. It makes sense, when both are taking advantage of the very same food source. However long they keep you company, make sure to notice all the possible correlation between the birds and the fish. Use the birds' visible behavior, concentrations, timing of peak intensity, and activity changes as likely indicators of trout activity. Logically, the behavior is driven by bug activity, so an angler is smart to pay close attention and determine which visible signs matter the most. Here are some examples:

- Gathering of swallows just off the lake generally indicates anticipated activity from the food source within a short time. If fish are inactive, expect the bite to start picking up soon.
- Early feeding and low flying to skim the surface likely means the majority of the hatch is still at depth. A cast-troll-retrieve-repeat approach with a full sink is a good method, as well as simply counting down longer. Chironomid fishers will go to a long-leader method here.
- More circular and erratic patterns of up and down flight suggest the concentration of food is at or near the surface, as more food is now being taken in the air. You probably know the answer already—shorter count and rip it back, or use a floating or slow sinking line.

When shade from the setting sun overtakes the lake surface, this is the time to be on the prowl. Rest assured more than a few hungry trout will be doing the same.

Other predators like eagles and osprey can be an indicator of active fish as well; however, they obviously don't show in great numbers, and they aren't pursuing the same foods fish consume. (They're competing with you and me for the fish!) Swallows show a more complex set of behaviors that can be used to monitor a food source they share with the trout and, ultimately, to make predictions about trout.

Also remember the less obvious clues like shade, surface chop, abrupt weather change, and other non-edible signs. And consider that fish are creatures of social habit and always look for an excuse to hang out with each other, whether food related or not. It's our job to always seek out that excuse, find the gathering, and exploit it until they hit the road for the next social event.

Other methods of finding concentrated fish may include watching fellow anglers, reading recent reports, or even using a fish finder, if you so choose. You have several good options, and none of them is wrong here. If you use one of these last three, just be mindful of the degree to which you lean on it. I would encourage anyone to advance toward the first set of methods I described for several very good reasons: Ultimately they are the most effective and will yield the best results by a long shot. You also won't get far in stillwater without those abilities to make sound observations, understand and interpret them, and convert all of the information into strikes. And making a habit out of leaning on others or a device will serve as a handicap in the long run, undermining your ability to seek out and follow clues for yourself. Most important of all, that exercise—of observation and the interpretation of natural clues that determine your approach—is the heart of our sport. If you miss that, you're not fishing. You're simply letting others, or a device, fish for you. To me, that's no better than sitting at home in front of a video game.

Decisions, Decisions

Throughout the day, you should be making them constantly. How you utilize time, where you locate, and the methods you use will be a constant part of your decision-making process as you work to solve the puzzle. One of the biggest things I struggle with every time out is the desire to try more than one thing at a time. I continually scrutinize my choices, wondering what's going on in other locations on the water, or what another method might yield if I were to change up. At times, it's rather tough to justify my choices as opposed to other alternatives, and occasionally I simply have to start somewhere and let the strikes, or lack thereof, determine what comes next.

In any case, it's more than a matter of simple trial-and-error whenever I'm torn between options. The problem is, I can make a strong argument for both. So the challenge becomes one of disciplining myself to actually choose the better of the two, when just guessing might work as well as anything. The idea here is to base your decisions on a logical thought process instead of flying blind, waiting for the strikes to lead you around. You *can* catch fish that way, but you'll catch a lot more by applying a thought process, establishing priorities, and making decisions based on those priorities. You won't always be right—I can attest to that—but by making well-thought-out decisions all day, you can keep learning and evolving in your approach according to what's working and what is not.

Simplify Somehow

In a sport that cannot be fully mastered in a mere lifetime, the notion of simplifying your approach is anything but intuitive. Yet there is a point where too much of a good thing is just that. Odd as it may sound, another good way to wear your net out faster is by narrowing down your game. This means there is such a thing as too much gear, too many flies, too many lakes and ponds on your list, too much water to effectively cover on a single lake, too many methods to keep track of, and so on. It's actually very easy to complicate the game so much that your ability to simply draw strikes becomes choked. Our attention spans only have so much capacity, and a day spent multitasking on the water only serves to distract an angler.

My recommendation is to become very effective at a few things instead of trying to master a large multitude. Trout really don't require an arsenal that big or a game plan that complicated. You're smart to find those few things that fit your style the best and then play to those strengths while letting the lower priorities go. For me, that meant narrowing my fly choices to a limited few, having only two fly lines, using the same rod and reel, frequenting only a half dozen lakes and ponds throughout the year (while visiting others less often), and holding my chosen methods to a handful while on the water. In making these choices, I allowed myself to focus on the priorities that matter most when I fish; namely, paying constant attention to WHEN and WHERE fish are active, along with HOW and WHAT to present to them for best results.

If I Were a Fish
This is almost a relative of simplification. One way we commonly choose to complicate things on the water is by humanizing the trout we pursue, thereby making him more sophisticated than he actually is—a lot more sophisticated. We purchase highly technical equipment and tie some very intricate and visually impressive flies just to chase a 12-inch creature with a brain the size of a pea, and who behaves solely on instinct. A trout does not reason or follow logic like you and I do. It has not acquired a taste for the finer things (or foods) in life. It also does not follow the news, enjoy good entertainment, maintain relationships, or even have a Facebook profile. So how are we so easily outfoxed by these creatures? For starters, it's not by any effort on their part. The problem lies solely with you and me, and our inclination to humanize fish, while failing to understand and play to their simplistic behavior. Beyond basic survival and propagation, there really isn't much to what drives trout in the course of a day. They need to feed and avoid predation, while conserving energy—and if we understand that much about their behavior, we have enough of the puzzle. Keep those

simple things in mind as you search for fish, and strikes will become surprisingly commonplace. The more you can dehumanize a trout, the more easily you can follow it around and draw its reaction.

ALSO WORTH KNOWING

Percentage Landed. In active conditions, don't be surprised to miss or lose a greater number of fish than you're used to. When fish are feeding aggressively, you'll often experience takes that are more abrupt. Drive-by strikes and swats are commonplace here, so once again, don't get hung up thinking you have a problem with technique. Instead, just enjoy all the action, and remind yourself that your take at day's end will still be a nice big number.

Applying Time Management. It's another recurring theme of mine, I know. In this case, a practical tip or two are worth keeping in mind. For one, during the busier parts of the day, just make sure you're hard at work; save the slower periods for breaks and such. *Callibaetis* hatches come to mind here. When they pop, the action is fast and furious on dry flies, but

True, at times of high activity you can expect to land a lower percentage of hookups. Although it's generally nothing to cry over, some fish would be heartbreaking for any angler to lose.

the duration is relatively short-lived. I hate even changing flies in the middle of one of these hatches. Every minute that goes by un-fished seems a terrible waste. Another tip—as each occurrence of feeding dies off, you'll want to find that balance between taking full advantage and lingering too long afterward. You're smart to think about getting them while you can, but when the strikes stop coming, be sure to closely regulate how long you stay there and hold out. You can get hurt if the opportunity cost is too great and if simply moving on would have put you back on good numbers of fish in short order.

Slow Action on Fast Days. Even during peak season, activity will ebb and flow throughout the day. At times, the majority of the day may be a little slow or dead altogether, an indication that the lake is currently hosting a very strong food source. This is your signal to identify the source-in-progress (if you don't already know it) and play hard to it.

Callibaetis and damsels are famous for this in spring and summer. Instinctively, the fish are keen on these as abundant food sources, and they know to lay off the rest of the day when feeding time is going to be significant enough to provide for the entire day. At these times, it is common to end the day with a lesser take. While the feed is on however, the action can be fast and furious. If you ask me, these days are well worth showing up for. And if you can key in on the approximate time and duration of an occurrence, you may even plan multi-lake outings around it.

I tend to have alternate locations close to most of my favorite haunts for this very reason. If I know a spot will light up at only one part of the day for a time, I'll often hit another lake or pond for that part of the day when the first lake is less active. I like this for staying on active fish for a longer period, and I am sometimes able to fish across several species in one day.

Change in Activity. One of the most common behaviors among anglers in reaction to a slowing of activity is to call it quits. The lake loves to empty out anytime a hatch or other food source cycles out during the day. But with few exceptions, when conditions are favorable, fish will continue to feed throughout the day, connecting the dots between food sources or even following changes within a single food source. A more prolific food source, such as midges, may occur for most of the day, and the manner in which fish feed on them may change several times.

In any case, whenever time allows, the obvious message here is to just stay put and continue solving a more complex puzzle that has a greater number of moving parts than it would in the off-season. A simple change in activity or behavior is just a small piece of that larger puzzle. If you take that as a sign that it's over for the day, chances are you'll only see a fraction of your potential take in that outing. And to go a step further, you should count on "starting over" a good half-dozen times a day, on average, at better times of year. That means continuing to find the next time, location, depth, and food source where fish are gathered each time you exhaust a hotspot. It rarely, if ever, happens that you can take fish all day using the same method, in the same location, on the same food source. It just doesn't work that way.

Multiple Food Sources. A couple of things are worth pointing out here. With a stronger food source, you should be able to find active fish—or come up with a good logical reason for no feeding that would suggest a solution. In other words, when fish are not active on a viable food, it can only be because a more desirable alternative exists. It follows that this alternative should be your solution to the current lack of strikes. For instance, say a fair number of midges have been showing throughout the morning. However, there is no visible activity among fish at surface, and your efforts to search the depths and various terrains are pretty much fruitless. It becomes obvious the fish just aren't interested and must have something else in mind. As it turns out, midges have been in hatch for several weeks now, and mayflies began showing about a week ago. So now something more filling is phasing in and beginning to pop in numbers. From previous discussion, we know that fish will instinctively key-in early and begin making the transition, even while the former food source remains stronger. The obvious solution here is to start abandoning the midges yourself and follow this early movement onto the new source. Note that a reduction in the amount of action you've been used to is a normal byproduct during these transitions. It's not you. Feeding may simply curtail for a time, as the fish adjust to the next dominant food source. And though activity tends to fluctuate over the life of each source, I usually find the busiest feeding to occur in the earlier part of the cycle. Once the fish fully transition over, feeding becomes quite aggressive—even well before the source hits its peak.

The other behavior worth watching for and understanding is the tendency fish have to adjust in the middle of a food's occurrence, and to become more efficient as consumers. Here you'll find them laying low the better part of the day, only to come out and feed for a short time when the food is most concentrated and abundant. In this way, they spend the least amount of energy and take the least amount of risk, while receiving the most benefit for their efforts. Tough on you and me as anglers, even worse when we don't see it and react to it. On the flip side, when we can identify the behavior and adjust accordingly, those periods when they come on will more than make up for the time spent waiting.

Responsible Handling. I know it's a tough problem to have once you start enjoying some success. With everything else to keep track of, it's easy to overlook the necessity of caring for the health and safety of the fish you come in contact with, assuming catch-and-release. On busy days, I always make it a point to slow down and take care of each one landed. The basic methods are still the same (i.e., proper handling and hook removal, using a net for larger fish, returning to the water ASAP, etc.). It's just that now you're handling a greater number of fish, so the tendency is to become a little careless or sloppy without meaning to. I say this because I know how we all are when the bite is on and that sense of urgency takes over. And since we're all normal and human, it requires some effort to remember some of those important details that involve taking care of the resource. For that matter, slowing down enough to treat your surroundings and fellow anglers with respect would also apply here. Same thing again—there really is no science or special method to it, just an awareness.

HUMAN BEHAVIOR

I know how much you enjoyed it in the last lesson, so I thought I'd do it again here. Only this time, let's look at some common behaviors among anglers when conditions are right and the bite is on. To reiterate, I'm not looking to call out poor fishing practices. The purpose here is to identify the stuff we have a normal tendency to do on the water, stuff that adversely affects results. All we're looking to do is break those common habits that get between you and the fish you're trying to catch. Note that some of these are repeats from the prior lesson. Only this time we are placing the same behavior in a different setting, in order to see the effects in better conditions.

Bliss. You're almost guaranteed to catch fish on certain days, and early on we talked about deciding which experience you wanted: hitting maybe 8 easy fish, or something closer to 40. Among other things, a big decider here is your willingness and ability to diligently observe, interpret, and react to clues. A lot of anglers on the water, some by choice and some not, will take that easy 8 and call it good. And again, there's absolutely nothing wrong with that. However, if your preference is to take those better days and claim a much greater number of trout, you'll need to fish as hard as any other day. Only now the rewards are multiplied, even hard to believe at times.

Ignorance. A subset of bliss, you can see this one every time out, as well. Simply put, ignorance is when an angler disregards the obvious signs that suggest he is on the wrong path at the moment. For example, the sun hangs brightly overhead, no visible signs of fish can be seen at surface, and midges can be seen distributed out across the lake. Regardless, you continue to work the shallows right against shore without a strike. Maybe you had luck there a week ago, or maybe you read a report that said fish were being nailed left and right along the banks. Whatever the reason, if the action and you are worlds apart, have a look around and see if anything glaring stands out that would explain the problem. If so, it may lead you to the solution (in this example, all three clues would lead you to try the depths next). Worst case, take a guess and at least move off that unproductive shoreline.

Assuming It's Over. One of the most popular human behaviors on the water. Maybe the bite was red hot for the last couple of hours, or perhaps they were hitting nonstop along shore while those damsels were coming up. In any case, they disappeared rather abruptly, so that must be it. Chances are, in better conditions, the action will shift and re-emerge several times throughout the day. If you ask me, the real fun and sport is in following that action around and figuring out their next move each time. In late spring, for example, I look at the puzzle as a series of smaller puzzles, each with its own individual solution. In solving as many of those small puzzles as I can, I am, in turn, solving the day's big puzzle.

Rolling Over. Similar to the above. However, here you've worked the place over since 7 a.m. without a single strike, and it's now going on eleven. That's enough. Surely they aren't biting today. Moon must be off or something. Here I'd refer to that rule of balancing we discussed before. Assuming you've been diligent in your approach and covered water effectively, that lack of activity in otherwise prime conditions should be a very strong sign of things to come. Solution: Stick around, grab lunch, and plan your attack for the afternoon. Depending on which month it is, you should have a reasonable idea of what the food source will be. And if the bite was dead-cold all morning, get ready for just the opposite that afternoon. Likely they're keyed in on something that occurs in great quantity in the latter part of the day. One other tip: Most times when I run across a situation like this, my total for the day ends up greater than I would have thought before showing up. That means that when they do finally come on, the action is intensely productive—to the degree that it more than makes up for a slow first half.

Dying on a Rock Over and Over. Same as before, only now fish can probably be found feeding in several situations over the course of the day. Consequently, several methods would be required to follow them around and stay in the strike zone as they shift. And so it goes. An angler who sticks to a predetermined method, or even a handful of them, without letting the fish or clues determine his choices, will likely miss out. Sadly, most or all of that abundant action would have been right in front of him the whole time.

Running Them Over. You guessed it. Only now you're killing more opportunity. I've watched a lot of anglers troll a short distance from shore, out where they should be. Then, on sight of activity against the bank, they'll turn inward and row along the shoreline, instead of changing methods and casting inward. Maybe the damsels brought these fish in, or perhaps a *Callibaetis* hatch. Could even be minnows. Fish will gather in tight for a number of reasons; joining the party with your pontoon and flapping oars is probably the fastest way to send them packing. Kiss a good observation and a great opportunity goodbye. And probably the most tragic part is,

Tale of two lines. Left side: Deadly stillwater weapon (Type V full sink). Right side: Common form of disarmament. Use that floater sparingly on lakes.

after a few minutes of trolling against shore unsuccessfully, anglers will simply return to the open and resume trolling there.

More Lime Green. If it's why folks get skunked on slow days, it's also why folks get a half-dozen on days when 40 or 50 would otherwise be commonplace. Stillwater's first and foremost rule: The majority of the time, if you use a floater, you're fishing *up here* while all the fish are *down there.* Unless you're taking them on drys or rigged for Chironomids, grab the full sink and get it down to them. Trust me on this one, when strikes are occurring at two to four feet of depth, you'll still get a lot more action on that sinker instead of with the lime-green approach. Same holds for casting against the bank.

When Trolling Really Hurts. Similar idea to floating lines. The more active the lake becomes, the more opportunity you miss out on by trolling. Wherever fish congregate to feed, you'll want the most direct and effective presentation that puts you in front of them, while drawing continued reaction for the duration of that feeding occurrence. The common human behavior here is continuing to troll while several obvious clues tip you off to all the activity. These may include visible food and feeding, strikes, or other anglers with bent rods. A lot of anglers will dismiss a strike as random or may "wise up" and troll back and forth through a possible zone. Even there, you can multiply your results by pinpointing the food source, location, and depth of strikes. Then work a concentrated area with the cast–count down–retrieve–repeat method. Again, you understand what these fish are feeding on, along with the location and depth, and are then going directly at them to draw a reaction with each cast. Big difference.

About Peer Pressure. Lots of fish generally means lots of fly fishers. Assuming you're not alone on the lake, the anglers around you provide a lot of useful information, spoken or otherwise. The common behavior here is either copying the wrong individuals or ignoring the right ones. Examples: If you observe six anglers all trolling with floating lines and getting little or nothing, I would advise against becoming the seventh. However, if you spot two anglers fishing together and cleaning house on a damsel hatch against shore, you'd be foolish not to get in on it. At the sight of success, folks choose not to follow suit for any number of reasons. They may lack the confidence or ability to execute in the same manner, they might not have the proper gear, they may be too set in their ways, or they could simply be too bashful to ask the necessary questions.

Whatever the reason, if that's you, figure out why, and then force yourself to overcome the issue. It doesn't even matter if you get it right at first. In fact, it may take several tries to nail down a change of method like that. Soon enough you will, and you want that ability to observe another angler, decipher his methods, and go to it yourself with the same success. Eventually you'll wear the other shoe, helping others crack the code, but for now, this is a very good step in getting there.

Must Be the Fly. Whether someone is hitting fish or not, the fly gets blamed nearly every time. And as you know, most of the talk that surrounds the taking of fish is about the fly being used. "Wha'd ya gettim on?" Good ice breaker, lousy information. On the other hand, finding out the food source—along with depth, location, and presentation style—will speak volumes about drawing strikes, far more than talking about the bait that happened to be on the hook. If anything, in terms of gear, I'm more interested in the line type being used when someone is hitting fish after fish.

Hint: Start making a habit of asking about line choice whenever you inquire about someone's luck and the fly they have on; and may I suggest answering that question the same way. Your fly line has much more to do with drawing strikes than any pattern ever will. In a high activity situation, you need to know where trout are concentrated; once you can get in front of them, you have quite a variety of fly choices that will work. It follows that keying in on the fly by itself will get you nowhere, or, at best, you'll hit a very small fraction of your potential. In giving the fly that much credit, you are selling yourself way short.

C&R (catch-and-release) without the C. Although better for the fish, releasing them prior to the catch is probably not your intended goal. The most common form of human error in playing fish is allowing slack in the line. There are other ways of giving them up, but this one seems to loom large in comparison. No matter how well you stuck him, a frantic trout on a barbless hook is difficult enough to keep engaged when played in textbook fashion. Give him slack while he darts and takes to the air, and you couldn't try any harder to shake him loose. And in spring, when trout are active and energetic, you'll give up a lot more by playing them carelessly. Once again, you've come a long way in coaxing this fish to strike. Why would you give him up so easily?

As you can imagine, each of the behaviors above comes at a much higher cost during the more productive parts of the year. And just as doing the right things all day can yield amazing results, doing some of the wrong things can hurt equally. Interestingly, each is rather simple, yet has a very high potential impact on your success. A great exercise is to start monitoring your decisions and methods throughout the day in terms of the numbers they yield. Then think of the items above in the same way. What's the potential cost of doing each in terms of forfeited fish? Hard to say, but by now you can see it's more than just one or two. For any single item, the number could be 10, or just as easily 20 or more.

The good news is that getting in the game and capitalizing on all that action require nothing more than a few changes of simple habit. All we're doing here is replacing a handful of less productive habits with more effective ones. And with these new ones, we're not talking about a ton of training or education. These are just different ways of thinking and acting as you pick your chosen lake apart. It may seem far away at first, but all that opportunity is a lot closer than you realize. You don't need difficult or sophisticated methods to take advantage, you just need the right, simple methods at the right times.

ADDING IT ALL UP

Now let's put this stuff into practice on an active day and see the effect on your results.

Conditions and Trends. Today will be mostly overcast, with light rain and an occasional sunbreak. Mild winds should give a slight surface break while allowing decent visibility for any activity. Low: 48 degrees F. High: 57 degrees F. Surface: 56 degrees F. It's the first week of May, and still no one has bothered to tell the weather that spring arrived several weeks ago. Tulips and daffodils finally got sick of waiting and did their thing, as did that *Callibaetis* hatch, now well underway. This year's modest mayfly hatch has proven to remain a secondary source of food, behind a longstanding midge hatch. Midges have been active since late February and now, over two months along, are still going strong despite all the talk of winding down. Most of today's outing will owe itself to this prolonged lifecycle of midges.

Midmorning (18 fish). With these longer days, first light comes rather early, and you already know the midges aren't popping in any number until later in the morning. As it is, this will be a long day, so you skip a few early ones and opt for a full night's rest. You put in around nine o'clock and start trolling toward the small shoal across the way. No farther than 20 yards, and your first strike comes unexpectedly at depth. First fish on, but right away it shakes free. You stay there and make a few deep casts. Nothing more, so you tuck that away and resume trolling to see if anything more will strike the same way. As nothing more happens, it seems you had a loner. Soon you arrive at your destination. As you look around, an occasional midge suggests the day's hatch isn't far off. No visual feeding yet, and you decide the outer shoal at depth is the next place to try. No hurry in finding the action, as it's still early—and you're fully aware of the day's potential once those midges are in bloom. For now, any success will be extra frosting.

Another bump comes at depth, but no hookup. Fine, you'll take the clue and keep grinding. Finally, your first fish takes it for good and you're no longer skunked. By now, five other anglers are on the lake, two anglers fishing Chironomids, two more trolling together with floaters, and another who just put in. First Chironomid guy is at the far end of the lake, so no idea if he's onto anything. The other is within sight, and neither he nor the two anglers trolling have had any luck yet. Just as your strategy becomes a continued scrape of that outer shoal, you begin seeing dimples out across the open water. One or two turn into several, and, as you look around, you start seeing a lot more midges breaking out. The sight is a much-welcome change, as you abandon the shoal floor and start looking to intercept some of these cruising trout. That brings success, and the next hour or so yields another six fish before the area cools off.

By eleven o'clock, you decide to put it deep again and make the commute to the far end, where bigger plans await. Within 100 yards or so, you get bumped, no hookup, and also see a few risers nearby. Five-minute test: you stop and make a few casts in a circle, counting down to various depths. Clearly, these fish are on a mission to rob you of valuable time, as none react to your offerings. Any concentration is likely to be nearer the shoal at the far end, so you commit to getting there without further delay. Fortunately, you pick up two more on the troll, and after spending 25 minutes commuting, you're grateful to arrive at the far end. Hopefully you can resume the real action.

The good news is, you've been here recently and just made a calculated move. Within a couple of hours, the mayflies will pop—and you're now in the vicinity of a very productive zone. But for now, good numbers of fish will occupy the surrounding area, either to stage for this hatch or to take advantage of heavy midge activity. You suspect a little of both. The first thing you notice is one of the anglers from before with rod bent. He's trolling a shallow section of the shoal, still with a floating line. You stay with your full sink and begin working shallow yourself. If these fish are concentrated, you should be able to hit a number of them with a cast-count-strip approach. At the same time, you keep the other angler in sight to test his method against yours. If he wins, you also win, as getting beat means someone just handed you a better method and gear choice. And if that happens, you'll gladly make the change.

As it turns out, you had it right. Your new friend picks up a second fish. You, on the other hand, land nine of your own before it cools down and you decide to start watching more closely for those mayflies.

Midday (3 fish). It's now nearing 1 p.m., and you nervously work the area out from shore, where you know that hatch is due any moment. You can't pinpoint the start of it each day, so changing spools too early would put you out of commission until they decide to start. On the other hand, wait too long and you'll frantically gear up while some of the oldest fish in the lake splash about, right in front of your face. You've done both, and consider the first scenario the lesser of two evils. You continue to cast but have your eyes firmly placed along that shoreline. Sure enough, that first one rolls, and you decide you've seen enough. Off come the gloves, and in short order, you're ready for the brawl. No bugs visible yet, but that's typical of these mayfly hatches. First sign you usually see is the behavior of hungry trout at the surface. The advantage here is having your fly on the water first, with little or no visible competition. In this circumstance, these fish are reacting to something highly visible sitting on top of the lake surface. That means your fly now matters a lot more than usual. From previous experience, you opt for a size #14 *Callibaetis* Emerger, your old standby. The choice works, as a well-placed first cast draws an early take. Unfortunately, your brain doesn't work so well. Once the fly was in place, you didn't expect anything that soon, so you weren't fully concentrating just yet. The wake-up call brought a premature hook set, and you know the rest.

OK, so now you're engaged, but that second strike is nowhere to be found. Typical, isn't it? You work away, following the rises around, casting in all the best places. But every time you move and cast, the action shifts. You know the pattern works, but it appears this year's hatch is already showing signs of early decline. You might be lucky to take one good fish from it today. As the fear of getting blanked sets in, you start moving and working faster. Finally a taker hits it against the overhang. Right away you know it's a small planter. Some of these have mixed in with the older rainbows and browns, seemingly to avoid feeding on midges in open water, which is not such a safe place for little fish. Nice to get something, but this is not exactly a fair trade for the midge action enjoyed earlier. The whole draw in working this mayfly hatch is the shot at an older fish, particularly a brown, on a dry fly. And you'll knowingly sacrifice a number of those open-water trout for one or two of these.

You continue to press on, as perseverance is the last available tool you have. Just out from your last one, another finally takes it down. Your timing is just right, and you set the hook on something worthwhile. It immediately comes toward you and heads for the bottom. Sure bet it's the brown you were looking for. Soon you get some lift and feel that the fish is fair-size but no monster. Finally, the 17-inch brownie is landed, and you're relieved to get paid off. After the release, you stay at it as the hatch winds down. You stick around for any stragglers and manage another planter before deciding it's over. Not a big take for one of these hatches, but with this one clearly on the decline, anything to the net is counted as success.

Midafternoon (18 fish). Going on 2:30 p.m., you decide to give the open another test before stopping for lunch. Near your takeout, a number of risers start showing. You look around some more and observe the thick part of the midge hatch has arrived. As you watch, the swallows take advantage all across the lake; you know for sure those fish are doing the same beneath the surface. Postponing lunch is probably the best choice for now, so you commit to dialing the action back in. As you start casting, you see more rises than you have all day. The feed has become more aggressive, yet nothing takes your offering as you work the upper end of the water column. Obviously the fish are there, and feeding is at its peak for the day.

Despite the facts, you opt to hold tight on method and fly selection. Past experience tells you a different fly won't cure this. These fish are displaying a common behavior that occurs when feeding is about to go into overdrive. You may encounter this momentary refusal, but soon they'll turn around and cooperate.

You convince yourself this is the proper solution and continue on. At about the time second-guessing sets in, here they come. First strike takes it hard and sticks and then another. Now the fun begins. You figure this flurry should get you to the 30-fish mark, and in fact, you get to 36 before any signs of slowing occur. By now you're 4 away from 40, and you attempt to press it before finally breaking for lunch. You're starving, but who knows what the lake will hold by the time you get back in. It would be nice to already have 40 before breaking, and why not milk this little flurry for everything? That idea gets you to 39, but then your wheels start spinning. Fine, better 39 than 36. It was worth it.

Late Afternoon/Early Evening (8 fish). Your late lunch comes and goes, and you jump back in, hoping for fish number 40 sooner rather than later. Difficult as it was to draw one more strike before lunch, you hit your first within minutes, as if the bite had never slowed. It even came in the same area using the same method. You proceed to put that area to another test but find it's time to move on. Trolling back to the near end of the lake, another one hits somewhere around midway. That one sticks, and you continue on, hoping for one or two more while in transit. Another bump is it, but before long, you arrive at the first shoal you worked this morning. You spot the occasional dimple out toward the middle but decide to work the immediate area, where they might be better concentrated. You'll go out there if nothing shows itself in close. The shoal and area just beyond the drop yield more fish, but it's a grind. Nothing shows in the upper column, but a diligent cast-troll-strip approach is producing some action. Six more come up, half on the troll and half on the retrieve, and then it slows once again. The weather has improved by now, and the sun is falling behind the trees. You decide to move farther out into the open, but the trail is cold out there. Perhaps the evening shade will liven up the shoal one more time.

Dusk/Takeout (5 fish). Early evening turns to dusk, and a short-lived flurry goes off. They don't seem area specific, but you figure any concentration would take place around that shoal or along the shoreline. Your work pays off with shallow casts bringing another four fish. Then you call it good and head for the truck. No surprise, one more calls from the depths as you troll across. That's plenty for one day. You're more than worn out, so no need for another search near the takeout.

Once again, let's add it up: $18 + 3 + 18 + 8 + 5 = 52$

All told, you wouldn't change anything. You figure the lake could have coughed up a middle-60s total—if you had shown at first light, as well as skipping the mayfly hatch in favor of the more productive midges. However, a couple of hours less sleep would have dampened the back half of this outing, and that brownie was worth every bit of effort and heartache spent in his pursuit. Fifty-two fish still sounds impressive, but a number by itself does not say much. Any take is still relative in terms of a specific lake, the conditions at hand, and a number of things that you will determine for yourself. Knowledge, experience, skill, and even your motivation that day are among them. And today you played your best game, while having a priority or two that kept the outcome from going any higher. Even in prime conditions like these, your objective will rarely, if ever, be to land every last fish possible. Instead, you put your best foot forward while making the outing serve you. You fished your very best, and tested yourself well as an angler. Let's list some of the ways you did this:

- You came to a familiar body of water with recent knowledge of its trends.
- You were patient, thorough, and methodical.
- You acted on your observations and made well-thought-out decisions.
- You were open to change.
- You used other anglers as a resource.
- You had to relearn a hard lesson about dry flies and paying attention. (Unfortunately, it won't be the last time!)
- You managed your time effectively.
- You kept a backup plan most of the day.

Today, little may have been learned in terms of anything new, but so many things from the past were nicely put into practice. This outing was one of reaping benefits, and as you can see, when conditions were prime, there was far more to the game than simply showing up and waiting for the action to come to you. If, on a slow day, you'll show a pretty good take when others are nearly skunked, here you'll be into numbers hard to believe, while others may end with a good handful at best.

Hopefully, these scenarios have brought to life some of the concepts introduced earlier. For what it's worth, the outings described were based on real situations and numbers. Again, it's all relative, so you can expect to see both better and worse out there as you encounter each new puzzle. And remember, with each puzzle, the solutions vary with the number of anglers trying their hands at it that day. Just as no two puzzles are alike, no two anglers will come up with the same solution for a single puzzle. Great if yours is among the best in terms of results. But the true measure of a solution is the amount of fun you had.

Index

Page numbers in italics indicate illustrations.